Janice VanCleave's

202

Oozing,
Bubbling,
Dripping,
and
Bouncing
Experiments

Other Titles of Interest from Wiley

Science for Every Kid Series
    Janice VanCleave's Astronomy for Every Kid
    Janice VanCleave's Biology for Every Kid
    Janice VanCleave's Chemistry for Every Kid
    Janice VanCleave's Dinosaurs for Every Kid
    Janice VanCleave's Earth Science for Every Kid
    Janice VanCleave's Ecology for Every Kid
    Janice VanCleave's Geography for Every Kid
    Janice VanCleave's Geometry for Every Kid
    Janice VanCleave's The Human Body for Every Kid
    Janice VanCleave's Math for Every Kid
    Janice VanCleave's Oceans for Every Kid
    Janice VanCleave's Physics for Every Kid

Spectacular Science Projects Series
    Janice VanCleave's Animals
    Janice VanCleave's Earthquakes
    Janice VanCleave's Electricity
    Janice VanCleave's Gravity
    Janice VanCleave's Machines
    Janice VanCleave's Magnets
    Janice VanCleave's Microscopes and Magnifying Lenses
    Janice VanCleave's Molecules
    Janice VanCleave's Rocks and Minerals
    Janice VanCleave's Volcanoes
    Janice VanCleave's Weather

    Janice VanCleave's 200 Gooey, Slippery, Slimy, Weird and Fun Experiments
    Janice VanCleave's 201 Awesome, Magical, Bizzarre & Incredible Experiments

Janice VanCleave's

202
Oozing, Bubbling, Dripping, and Bouncing Experiments

John Wiley & Sons, Inc.

New York · Chichester · Brisbane · Toronto · Singapore

Copyright © 1996 by Janice VanCleave
Published by John Wiley & Sons, Inc.

Portions of this book have been reprinted from the books *Janice VanCleave's Animals*, *Janice VanCleave's Astronomy for Every Kid*, *Janice VanCleave's A+ Projects in Chemistry*, *Janice VanCleave's Biology for Every Kid*, *Janice VanCleave's Chemistry for Every Kid*, *Janice VanCleave's Dinosaurs for Every Kid*, *Janice VanCleave's Earthquakes*, *Janice VanCleave's Earth Science for Every Kid*, *Janice VanCleave's Electricity*, *Janice VanCleave's Gravity*, *Janice VanCleave's The Human Body for Every Kid*, *Janice VanCleave's Machines*, *Janice VanCleave's Magnets*, *Janice VanCleave's Math for Every Kid*, *Janice VanCleave's Molecules*, *Janice VanCleave's Physics for Every Kid*, *Janice VanCleave's Volcanoes*, and *Janice VanCleave's Weather*.

The publisher and the author have made every reasonable effort to ensure that the experiments and activities in this book are safe when conducted as instructed but assume no responsibility for any damage caused or sustained while performing the experiments or activities in this book. Parents, guardians, and/or teachers should supervise young readers who undertake the experiments and activities in this book.

Library of Congress Cataloging-in-Publication Data

VanCleave, Janice Pratt.
   Janice VanCleave's 202 oozing, bubbling, dripping, and bouncing
experiments / Janice VanCleave.
      p.   cm.
   Includes index.
   Summary: Provides instructions for over 200 short experiments in
astronomy, biology, chemistry, earth science, and physics.
   ISBN 0-471-14025-2 (pbk. : alk. paper)
   1. Science—Experiments—Juvenile literature.   2. Scientific
recreations—Juvenile literature.   [1. Science—Experiments.
2. Experiments.]   I. Title.
Q164.V44   1996
507.8—dc20   95-46398

Printed in the United States of America

10   9   8   7   6   5   4   3   2   1

Dedication

It is my pleasure to dedicate this book to a special lady who has enriched my life with her bouncy, bubbly personality. What fun I have had exchanging ideas over the years with my friend, Dorothy Maynard.

Acknowledgments

A special note of thanks for their support and a word of encouragement to the following young budding scientists and their adult helpers:

- Kenneth and Dianne Fleming
- Robert, Kymie, Krysti, Alan, Megan, and Clayton Hooper
- Kenneth Roy, Kim, Brittany, and Bradley Fleming
- Robert, Heather, Austin, and April Fleming
- Brenda and Jacques Verron
- Carole, Amber, and Erin Pratt
- Robert and Mariete Haskett
- Jim, Connie, Jimmy, Robert, and Christine Ridgway
- Kenneth, Mary, and Christopher Haskett
- Eric Botot
- Ross, Cathy and Levi Cook

Contents

Introduction

This book is a collection of science experiments designed to show you that science is more than a list of facts—science is fun! The 202 experiments in the book take science out of the laboratory and put it into your daily life.

Science is a way of solving problems and discovering why things happen the way they do. Why does the moon shine? What causes an earthquake? How does sound travel? You'll find the answers to these and many other questions by doing the experiments in this book.

The experiments cover five different fields of science:

- **Astronomy** The study of the planets, the stars, and other bodies in space.
- **Biology** The study of the way living organisms behave and interact.
- **Chemistry** The study of the way materials are put together and their behavior under different conditions.
- **Earth Science** The study of the earth.
- **Physics** The study of energy and matter and their relationship.

The Experiments

Scientists identify a problem, or an event, and seek solutions, or explanations, through research and experimentation. A goal of this book is to guide you through the steps necessary to successfully complete a science experiment and to teach you the best method of solving problems and discovering answers.

1. **Purpose:** The basic goals for the experiment.
2. **Materials:** A list of necessary supplies.
3. **Procedure:** Step-by-step instructions on how to perform the experiment.
4. **Results:** An explanation stating exactly what is expected to happen. This is an immediate learning tool. If the expected results are achieved, the experimenter has an immediate positive reinforcement. An error is also quickly recognized, and the need to start over or make corrections is readily apparent.
5. **Why?** An explanation of why the results were achieved is described in terms that are understandable to the reader, who may not be familiar with scientific terms. When a new term is introduced and explained, it appears in **bold** type; these terms can also be found in the Glossary.

You will be rewarded with successful experiments if you read each experiment carefully, follow the steps in order, and do not substitute materials.

General Instructions

1. **Read first.** Read each experiment completely before starting.
2. **Collect needed supplies.** You will experience less frustration and more fun if you gather all the necessary materials for the experiments before you begin. You lose your train of thought when you have to stop and search for supplies.
3. **Experiment.** Follow each step very carefully, never skip steps, and do not add your own. Safety is of the utmost importance, and by reading the experiment before starting, then following the instructions exactly, you can feel confident that no unexpected results will occur.
4. **Observe.** If your results are not the same as described in the experiment, carefully read the instructions and start over from the first step.

Measurements

Measuring quantities described in this book are intended to be those commonly used in every kitchen. When specific amounts are given, you need to use a measuring instrument closest to the described amount. The quantities listed are not critical, and a variation of very small amounts more or less will not alter the results. Approximate metric equivalents are given in parentheses.

I
Astronomy

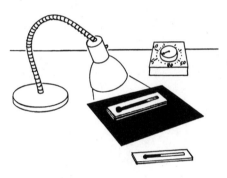

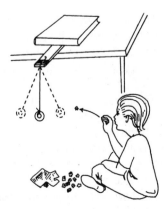

1. Bent

Purpose To demonstrate how the thickness of an atmosphere affects how light is bent.

Materials   modeling clay   2 shiny pennies
                2 drinking cups   tap water

Procedure

1. Stick a grape-sized piece of clay inside the bottom of each cup.
2. Press a penny in each piece of clay so that it is in the very center of the cup.
3. Fill one cup with water.
4. Place both cups on the edge of a table. The cups must be side by side and even with the edge of the table.
5. Stand close to the table. Then, take a few steps backward while observing the pennies in the cups.
6. Stop when you can no longer see either of the pennies.

Results The penny in the cup filled with air disappears from view first, while you can still see the penny in the cup filled with water.

Why? You see the penny in the water at a greater distance because light enters the cup, reflects from the penny, hits the surface of the water, and is **refracted** (bent) toward your eye. The water is thicker than the air and thicker materials refract the light more. A change in the thickness of the earth's **atmosphere** (the gases around a planet) due to pollution, increases the refraction of light. Venus' thick atmosphere refracts light much more than does the earth's atmosphere. An observer on Venus would see many **mirages** (optical illusions due to atmospheric conditions) and distortions because of this.

2. Rotate

Purpose To demonstrate one method of proving that the earth rotates.

Materials   9-inch (22.5-cm) piece of string
                washer
                pencil
                quart (liter) wide-mouthed glass jar
                ruler
                2 rolls of 2-inch (5-cm)-wide masking tape
                turntable

Procedure

1. Tie one end of the string to the washer, and the other end to the center of the pencil.
2. Place the pencil across the mouth of the jar so that the washer hangs in the center, about 2 inches (5 cm) from the bottom.
3. Place one roll of tape in the center of the turntable, and center the jar on the tape.
4. Gently turn the turntable.
5. Adjust the position of the jar and pencil so that the string hangs straight down as the turntable spins.
6. Stop the turntable and use the other roll of tape to tape the pencil so that it does not move.
7. Tilt the jar and place it back on the tape so that the washer swings back and forth.
8. Turn the turntable again at the same speed as before and observe the movement of the washer.

Results The washer continues to swing back and forth in the same direction even though the jar is rotating.

Why? **Inertia** is the resistance to any change in motion. An object in motion has a tendency to remain in motion. The washer keeps swinging in the same direction because of its inertia. A pendulum suspended and swung at the North Pole of the earth would continue to swing back and forth, while the earth beneath **rotates** (spins on its axis), making one complete turn in 24 hours.

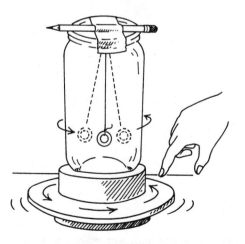

3. Heat Shield

Purpose To determine how space acts as a heat shield.

Materials quart (liter) wide-mouthed glass jar with a
lid
warm tap water
2 thermometers
thermos
2 drinking cups
timer

Procedure
1. Fill the jar with warm tap water.
2. Place one of the thermometers in the jar for 2 minutes.
3. Read and record the temperature of the water.
4. Pour half of the water from the jar into the thermos, then close the lids on the thermos and the jar.
5. Allow the thermos and the jar to sit undisturbed for 1 hour.
6. Open the jar and the thermos. Fill one of the cups with water from the thermos and fill the second cup with water from the jar.
7. Place one thermometer in each of the cups.
8. Wait 1 minute, then read and record the temperature of the water in each cup.

Results The temperature of the water inside the thermos changes less than does the temperature of the water inside the glass jar.

Why? Between the inside and outside of the thermos is a partial **vacuum** (space with nothing in it). Heat has difficulty traveling through a vacuum; thus, the vacuum acts as a heat shield. The partial vacuum separating **celestial** (of the heavens or sky) bodies is called **space**. Materials that allow heat to move through them are called **conductors**. Like the partial vacuum in the thermos, space is a poor conductor. Thus space acts as a shield, protecting celestial bodies from solar heat.

4. Rings

Purpose To determine what causes Saturn's rings.

Materials 3 sharpened pencils
masking tape
drawing compass
stiff cardboard, such as the back of a
writing tablet
scissors
cookie sheet
salt
adult helper

Procedure
1. Tape two of the pencils together so that their points are even.
2. Use the compass to draw a circle with an 8-inch (20-cm) **diameter** (length of a straight line passing through the center of the circle with both endpoints on the circle) on the cardboard.
3. Cut out the circle and have an adult use the point of the compass to punch a hole in the center.
4. Place the circle of cardboard, with the rough side of the hole down, on the cookie sheet.
5. Evenly cover the surface of the cardboard with salt.
6. Ask your helper to stand the third pencil point-down in the hole in the cardboard circle.

7. Rest the points of the taped pencils against the cardboard as your helper spins the cardboard around one full turn.

Results As your helper turns the cardboard circle, the pencil points push the salt to the side, forming two cleared paths.

Why? Saturn's rings are made of icy particles. Just as the pencil points move through the salt crystals in this experiment, astronomers believe that Saturn's moons move through the icy particles, pushing them into separate bands. These moons are called shepherd **satellites** (a small body that revolves around a larger body). The moons are given this name because they herd the icy particles in the rings.

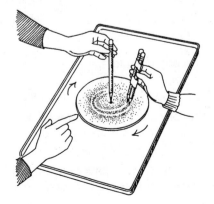

5. Farthest

Purpose To demonstrate how Neptune sometimes becomes the outermost planet.

Materials scissors   6 pushpins
                       ruler   pencil
                       string
                       sheet of typing paper
                       bulletin board (thick cardboard will work)

Procedure

1. Cut a 12-inch (30-cm) piece of string and tie the ends together to form a loop.
2. Secure the paper to the bulletin board with four of the pushpins.
3. In the middle of the paper, draw a line ½ inch (1.25 cm) shorter than the length of the loop and stick a pushpin into the bulletin board at each end of the line. Loop the string around the pushpins.
4. Place the pencil so that its point is inside the loop.
5. Keep the string taut as you guide the pencil around the inside of the string to draw an **ellipse** (oval) on the paper.
6. Cut a second piece of string 8 inches (20 cm) long.
7. Repeat steps 1 through 5 with the 8-inch (20-cm) string to draw a smaller ellipse inside the larger one.
8. Move the pushpins until you can draw a small ellipse

inside the larger one with one end of the small ellipse overlapping the larger one.

Results Two overlapping ellipses are drawn.

Why? The **orbit** (path of an object around another body) of each planet has an elliptical shape. Pluto, represented by the longer string, is usually the outermost planet in the solar system. During its journey around the sun, however, Pluto moves inside Neptune's orbit for a period of time, making Neptune the outermost planet. The two planets do not collide, because Pluto's orbit is above Neptune's.

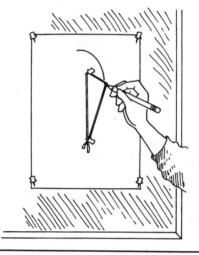

6. In Place

Purpose To demonstrate the point of balance between the earth and the moon.

Materials compass   pushpin
                       ruler   pencil
                       wax paper   black marker
                       scissors   modeling clay

Procedure

1. Use the compass to draw a circle with about a 4-inch (10-cm) diameter from the wax paper. Cut out the circle.
2. Stick the pushpin through the center of the circle and into the side of the eraser on the pencil.
3. Use the marker to make a black dot on the pencil ½ inch (1.25 cm) inside the edge of the paper circle.
4. Stick a grape-sized piece of clay on the point of the pencil.
5. Rotate the paper circle and observe the position of the black dot.
6. Hold the circle still and rotate the pencil.

Results The black dot always stays between the center of the paper circle and the clay ball, about ½ inch (1.25 cm) inside the edge of the paper.

Why? In your model, the paper circle represents the earth and the ball of clay represents the moon. **Gravi-**

tation (mutual attraction between objects) keeps the earth and moon together so that they act as a single body rotating around the sun. Your model uses a pencil to hold the paper earth and the clay moon together. The dot on the pencil represents the **center of gravity** (balancing point) of our earth-moon system, called the **barycenter**. The barycenter is the point that maps out the path of the earth-moon system around the sun. The model shows that the barycenter is not a definite place on the surface of the earth, but a point about 2,720 miles (4,352 km) below the earth's surface on the side facing the moon.

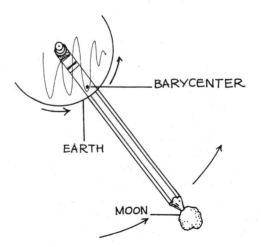

7. Moving Target

Purpose To simulate aiming a spacecraft for the moon.

Materials scissors   washer
                  ruler   book
                  string   paper towel
                  masking tape

Procedure

1. Cut a 24-inch (60-cm) piece of string.
2. Tape one end of the string to one end of the ruler.
3. Tie the washer to the free end of the string.
4. Place the ruler on a table with about 4 inches (10 cm) of the ruler extending over the edge of the table.
5. Place a book on top of the ruler to secure it to the table.
6. Tear and wad up 10 grape-sized pieces of the paper towel.
7. Pull the hanging washer to the side and release it to start it swinging.
8. Sit about 1 yard (1 m) from the swinging washer.
9. Pitch one wad of paper at a time at the moving washer.
10. Record the number of paper wads that hit the swinging washer.

Results The paper wads hit the washer when aimed at a point *in front* of the swinging washer.

Why? It takes time for the paper wads to move through the air. While they move, the washer moves to another position. Astronauts have the same problem when aiming their spacecraft at the moon because the moon, like the washer, is constantly changing positions. The paper wads and the spacecraft must be directed to a point in front of the moving target so that they arrive at the same place at the same time.

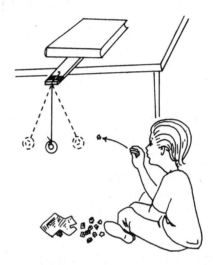

8. Eclipse

Purpose To demonstrate a solar eclipse.

Materials pen
                  poster board
                  timer
                  helper

Procedure

CAUTION: Never look directly at the sun. It can damage your eyes.

1. Use the pen to draw the largest possible circle on the poster board.
2. Mark an X at one point on the outline of the circle.
3. Place the poster board on the ground in a sunny area outside.
4. Stand in the center of the paper, facing the X. Ask your helper to make a mark on the paper where the center of your shadow crosses the circle.
5. Repeat the previous step every 30 minutes, six or more times during the day.

Results Your shadow crossed the circle at different points during the day.

Why? A **shadow** is a dark shape cast upon a surface when something blocks light. You cast a shadow because your body blocks the sun's light. During an **eclipse**, one object passes through the shadow of another. A **solar eclipse** occurs when the earth moves into the moon's shadow. At such times, the moon lies between the sun and the earth. The moon's shadow, like your shadow, falls on different areas of the earth because the earth **rotates**.

9. Darker

Purpose To determine why some areas of the earth are darker during a solar eclipse.

Materials sheet of typing paper
flashlight
ruler

Procedure
1. Lay the paper on a table.
2. Hold the flashlight about 14 inches (35 cm) from the paper.
3. Place your hand between the light and the paper about 1 inch (2.5 cm) above the paper.
4. Spread your fingers apart.
5. Observe the color of the shadow made by your hand on the paper.

Results The shadow is darker in the center than on the outside.

Why? Your hand casts a **shadow** because light traveling in a straight line from the flashlight is blocked by your hand. Light cannot pass through your hand; therefore, a dark shape or shadow appears on the paper. A shadow has two parts—the umbra and the penumbra. The **umbra** is the dark inner part of a shadow where the light is completely cut off. During a **solar eclipse**, the umbra of

the moon's shadow falls on a small part of the earth. The **penumbra** is the outer, lighter part of the shadow where the light is only partly cut off. The penumbra of the moon's shadow falls on a larger part of the earth during a solar eclipse.

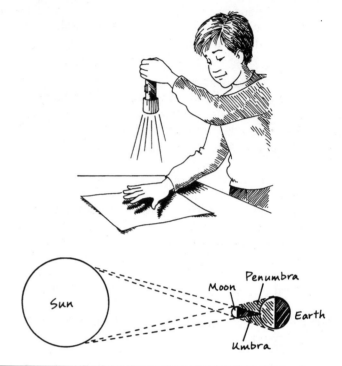

10. Blocked

Purpose To demonstrate a lunar eclipse.

Materials baseball   flashlight
several books   golf ball

Procedure
1. Place the baseball on a table.
2. Stack some of the books about 12 inches (30 cm) from the baseball.
3. Lay the flashlight on the books and point it toward the baseball. If the light doesn't shine directly on the baseball, raise or lower the flashlight by increasing or decreasing the number and/or size of books used.
4. Hold the golf ball to the side of the baseball.
5. Slowly move the golf ball behind the baseball (the side opposite the flashlight).

Results A dark shadow from the baseball falls across the golf ball as the golf ball moves behind the baseball.

Why? A **lunar eclipse** occurs when the moon moves into the earth's **shadow**. At such times, the earth lies between the sun and the moon. In this experiment, the baseball represents the earth, the flashlight represents the sun, and the golf ball represents the moon. As the moon moves into the shadow of the earth, the part of

the moon covered by the shadow is no longer visible. Finally, the entire moon seems to disappear. The reverse happens as the moon moves out of the earth's shadow.

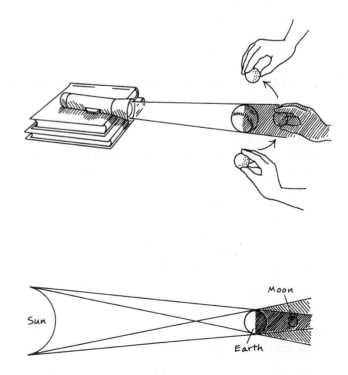

11. Which Way?

Purpose To make a shadow compass.

Materials pen   pencil
           paper plate

Procedure

CAUTION: Never look directly at the sun. It can damage your eyes.

1. Use the pen to mark the directions N, S, E, and W on the edge of the paper plate.
2. In the afternoon, lay the paper plate on the ground in a sunny area.
3. Push the point of the pencil through the center of the plate and into the ground about 1 inch (2.5 cm).
4. Move the pencil around until it no longer casts a shadow on the plate.
5. Wait until a shadow appears on the plate, then rotate the plate so that the shadow points toward the letter E.

Results The plate is turned so the letters on the plate point in the general compass directions of north, south, east, and west.

Why? When you point the end of the pencil straight at the sun, no **shadow** appears on the paper. The sun appears to move in a general direction from east to west. As it moves toward the west, the sun's light hits the pencil, forming a **shadow** pointing toward the east. Rotating the plate so that the letter E lines up with the shadow places all the letters in line with the compass directions of north, south, east, and west. Any general direction can then be determined from the shadow compass. (If you had performed the experiment before noon, you would have rotated the plate so that the letter W lined up with the shadow.)

12. Where Is It?

Purpose To determine the position of the sun in the sky.

Materials yardstick (meterstick)
modeling clay
protractor
1-yard (1-m) piece of string
sharpened pencil
helper

Procedure

CAUTION: Never look directly at the sun.

1. Place the measuring stick on an outside table. Point one end toward the sun.
2. Use the clay to stand the protractor upright against the side of the measuring stick, with its center at the end of the stick.
3. Tie one end of the string around the pencil point. Stand the pencil on the measuring stick.
4. Move the pencil back and forth until the shadow of the pencil point strikes the end of the stick.
5. Ask your helper to pull the string to the end of the measuring stick and to read the angle where it crosses the protractor.
6. Repeat steps 4 and 5 at different times.

Results The angle reading varies with the time of day.

Why? Each day the sun appears to rise from below the eastern **horizon** (a line where the earth and sky appear to meet). It then moves across the sky and sinks below the western horizon. The **altitude** (height) of the sun changes during the day. At sunrise and sunset, the altitude is zero degrees. Each day the greatest altitude is around noon. During the year, the sun's greatest altitude is during the summer. Its lowest altitude is during the winter.

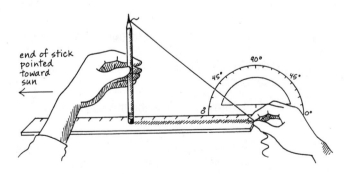

end of stick pointed toward sun

13. Spots

Purpose To simulate the magnetic field around spots on the sun.

Materials rubber gloves (the kind used for dishwashing)
scissors
soapless steel wool pad (purchase at a variety store in the paint section)
1-teaspoon (5-ml) measuring spoon
small round magnet
sheet of typing paper

Procedure

1. Put on the gloves and use the scissors to cut very tiny pieces from the steel wool pad. The smaller the pieces, the better. Cut enough pieces to fill the measuring spoon.

   CAUTION: Do not remove the gloves. They prevent the steel wool from damaging your skin.

2. Place the magnet on a wooden table and cover it with the paper.
3. Sprinkle the steel wool pieces on the paper above the magnet.

Results The steel wool pieces form a pattern on the paper above the magnet.

Why? A **magnetic field** is the area around a magnet in which the force of the magnet affects the movement of other magnetic objects, such as steel wool. This area is made up of invisible lines of magnetic force. The small pieces of steel wool follow the lines of force, allowing you to "see" the magnetic field. Magnetic fields exist on the sun. Dark spots on the sun where gases are cooler are called **sunspots**. Like magnets, the sunspots are surrounded by magnetic fields that attract magnetic materials.

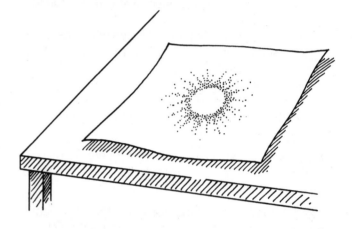

14. Direct

Purpose To determine why Mars and the earth both have cold poles.

Materials book
masking tape
2 sheets of black construction paper
2 thermometers

Procedure

1. Place the book on a flat surface in the sun.
2. Tape one piece of black paper on each side of the book.
3. Turn the book so that one sheet of paper receives direct sunlight.
4. Tape a thermometer on top of each sheet of black paper.
5. Read the temperature on both thermometers after 10 minutes.

Results The thermometer facing the sun has a higher temperature.

Why? The black paper facing the sun receives more direct rays of sunlight than the sheet on the opposite side of the book. Areas that receive direct light rays from the sun are much hotter. The earth's equator receives about 2½ times as much heat during the year as does the area around the poles. Mars, like the earth, has colder pole areas. Both of these planets are slightly tilted in their relationship to the sun, causing the center to receive more direct solar light rays than do the poles.

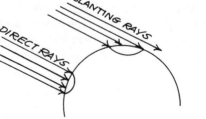

15. Sun Size

Purpose To calculate the diameter of the sun.

Materials pencil
sheet of typing paper
metric ruler
index card

straight pin
masking tape
meterstick
adult helper

Procedure

CAUTION: Never look directly at the sun.

1. Use the ruler to draw two parallel lines 2 mm apart on the sheet of paper.
2. Ask an adult to punch a hole in the center of the index card with the pin.
3. Fold over 1 cm of one short end of the index card. Tape the folded edge to the zero end of the meterstick.
4. Stand the meterstick outside in a sunny area and hold the sheet of paper at the 218-mm mark.
5. Adjust the stick and paper so that the shadow of the card falls on the paper and the circle of light fills the space between the lines you drew.

Results The circle of light fits between the lines. Thus, it has a 2-mm diameter.

Why? The distance from the hole in the card to the paper (218 mm) divided by the **diameter** of the circle (2 mm) equals 109. Thus, the distance of 218 mm divided by 109 equals the diameter of the circle. Astronomers have determined that an approximate diameter of the sun can also be calculated by dividing the distance from the sun to the earth (150,000,000 km) by 109. Thus, the diameter of the sun is about 1,376,147 km.

16. Moonbeams

Purpose To compare your speed to the speed of moonlight.

Materials 2 pencils
stopwatch
yardstick (meterstick)
2 helpers

Procedure
1. Lay one of the pencils on the ground to mark a starting line.
2. Have a trial run to determine about how far you can run in 4 seconds. Stand at the starting line. Ask one helper, called the "marking helper," to stand to the side and about 7 yards (6.4 m) in front of the starting line.
3. When your second helper, called the "timer," says "Start," run forward as fast as you can.
4. When the timer says "Stop" (at the end of 4 seconds), the marking helper lays a pencil at your location, and you stop as soon as possible.
5. Rest, then have a real run by repeating steps 2 through 4.
6. Use the measuring stick to measure the distance. Round the distance to the nearest yard (meter).
7. Divide the distance by 3.

Results Dividing the distance you traveled by 3 tells you the distance you traveled in one-third the time, or 1⅓ seconds. The result for the author of this book was 7 yards (6.4 m) in 1⅓ seconds.

Why? 1⅓ seconds is the length of time it takes for light to travel from the moon to the earth. The author of this book raced across her yard at a speed of 7 yards (6.4 m) in 1⅓ seconds while moonbeams of light traveled about 420,000,000 yards (384,000,000 m) to the earth in the same amount of time.

17. Shiner

Purpose To demonstrate why the moon shines.

Materials bicycle reflector
flashlight

Procedure
1. Do this experiment at night.
2. Point the flashlight at the bicycle reflector.
3. Turn the flashlight off.

Results The reflector glows only when the flashlight is on.

Why? The flashlight is **luminous** (gives off its own light). The reflector is not luminous, meaning it does not give off its own light. It is designed to reflect light from other sources in different directions. The moon, like the reflector, is not luminous. The moon reflects light from the sun. Without the sun, there would be no moonlight.

18. Heavy

Purpose To simulate the effect of the moon's gravity on weight.

Materials 24-inch (60-cm) piece of string
rock, about the size of a small apple
rubber band
large cooking pot or bucket
tap water

Procedure
1. Tie one end of the string around the rock and attach the other end of the string to the rubber band.
2. Place the pot on a table and set the rock inside.
3. Hold the free end of the rubber band and gently lift the rock just above the bottom of the pot.
4. Observe the length of the rubber band.
5. Fill the pot with water and repeat steps 3 and 4.

Results The rubber band stretched less when the rock was raised in water.

Why? **Gravity** (force that pulls toward the center of the earth) pulls the rock down, causing the attached rubber band to stretch. But when water is added to the pot, the water pushes up on the rock, canceling some of the downward pull of gravity. Raising the rock in the water simulates the effect of the moon's gravity on weight. The moon's gravity is only one-sixth as strong as the gravity on the earth.

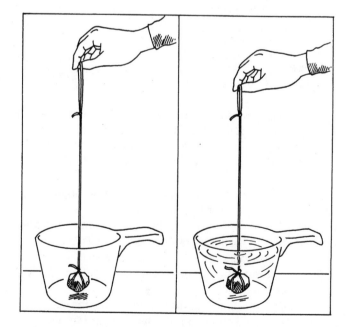

19. Plop!

Purpose To determine the type of surface where craters are best formed.

Materials 8-inch (20-cm) square of aluminum foil
newspaper
1 golf ball-sized rock

Procedure

1. Lay the newspaper on the carpet.
2. Lay one foil square on top of the newspaper.
3. Stand at the edge of the foil.
4. Hold the rock waist high and drop it in the center of the foil.
5. Repeat steps 1 through 4 on a hard floor.
6. Examine both pieces of foil.

Results The rock made a larger impression on the foil lying on the soft carpet.

Why? The rock sank into the softer carpet surface, which allowed more of the ball to be pressed against the paper. Like the rock, a **meteorite** (a stony or metallic object from space that falls through an atmosphere and strikes the surface of a celestial body) makes a larger imprint when it strikes a soft surface. Bowl-shaped holes called **craters** are best formed when meteorites strike soft, powdery surfaces such as the surface of the moon.

20. Splatter

Purpose To determine why moon craters are spread out.

Materials 2 cups (500 ml) soil   spoon
2-quart (2-liter) bowl   plate
tap water   4–6 pebbles

Procedure

1. Pour the soil into the bowl. Add small amounts of water, stirring continuously, until a muddy mixture forms.
2. Fill the plate with the mud mixture. Shake the plate to smooth out the surface of the mud.
3. Drop each pebble, one at a time, from a height of about 24 inches (60 cm) above the plate.
4. Move your hand so that the pebbles hit different areas of the mud's surface.

Results Each pebble produces a splatter of liquid and craterlike indentations on the surface.

Why? The falling pebbles simulate **meteorites**. The tremendous amount of heat produced by the impact of large meteorites melts the surface, and the liquid surface splatters, as did the mud. The decreased **gravity** on the moon allows the liquid to be blown higher and over a larger area. Thus the rims of many of the craters on the moon overlap, and the craters are separated by rough areas where thin layers of the liquid have fallen on the surface.

21. Too Much

Purpose   To determine why the moon's daytime temperature is so high.

Materials   sheet of black construction paper
desk lamp
2 thermometers
timer

Procedure

1. Lay the paper under the lamp.
2. Place one thermometer on the paper and position the lamp about 4 inches (10 cm) from its bulb.
3. Place the second thermometer away from the lamp.
4. Turn on the lamp and record both temperatures after 5 minutes.

Results   The reading on the thermometer under the lamp is much higher than on the other thermometer.

Why?   The moon's daytime temperature is about 266 degrees Fahrenheit (130°C). This is because the sun shines on the moon's surface continuously for about two earth weeks. There is also very little protection from the solar rays because the moon's **gravity** is so weak that a protective **atmosphere** cannot be captured as it is around the earth. Therefore, the sun heats the surface to

temperatures above the boiling point of water. While the sunny side is cooking, like the thermometer under the lamp, the shaded side is exposed to very cold space. (The second thermometer is not exposed to the cold, but it is cooler.) The shady side of the moon cools to about −279.4°F (−173°C).

22. Brightest Star

Purpose   To locate the brightest star.

Materials   compass

Procedure

CAUTION: *Never look directly at the sun.*

1. Just before sunrise, go outside and find a good view of the sky above the horizon.
2. Use the compass to determine the directions of east and west.
3. Face the east and look for a very bright star in the sky above the horizon.
4. If you don't see the star at sunrise, look for it above the western horizon after sunset.

Results   What appears to be a very bright star is usually seen in the morning before sunrise or in the evening after sunset. Sometimes the star is not visible.

Why?   The brightest star in the sky is not really a star, but the planet Venus. It appears as a bright star because the dense, unbroken clouds surrounding the planet reflect about 75 percent of the incoming sunlight back into space. The movement of the planet around the sun, as seen from the earth, makes it appear as an "evening" or "morning" star. It appears in the evening in

the western sky when moving toward the earth. It is in the eastern sky in the morning after it has passed between the sun and the earth and begins moving away from the earth. If the star is too close to the sun, the brightness of the sun blocks out the light from Venus and it cannot be seen.

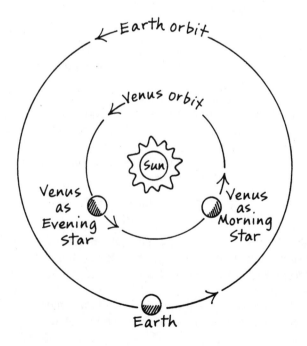

23. Twinkling Star

Purpose To simulate twinkling stars.

Materials 12-by-12-inch (30-by-30-cm) square of
aluminum foil
2-quart (2-liter) glass bowl
tap water
flashlight
pencil

Procedure
1. Crumple the foil with your hands. Open up the crumpled foil and place it on a table.
2. Fill the bowl with water and place it on top of the foil.
3. Darken the room and hold the flashlight about 12 inches (30 cm) above the bowl.
4. Gently tap the surface of the water with the pencil.
5. Observe the foil through the moving water.

Results Light reflecting from the foil appears to twinkle.

Why? The up-and-down movement of the water causes the depth of the water to vary. Light rays reflecting from the foil twinkle because they **refract**, or bend, differently as they pass through different depths of water. To an observer on earth, light rays from distant stars appear to twinkle because they also **refract** differently

as they move through different thicknesses of air in the earth's atmosphere. This twinkling or motion of starlight is called **scintillation**.

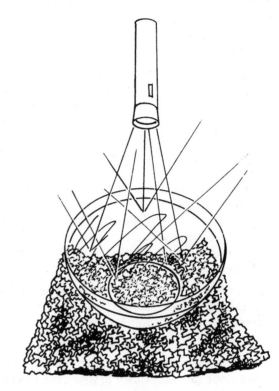

24. Star Projector

Purpose To make a star projector.

Materials round box, such as an empty oatmeal box
drawing compass
sheet of black construction paper
scissors
rubber band
chalk
flashlight
adult helper

Procedure
1. Ask an adult to remove both ends of the box.
2. Use the compass to draw a circle on the paper 2 inches (10 cm) wider than the end of the box.
3. Cut out the circle and place it over one end of the box. Secure the paper with the rubber band.
4. Use the chalk to draw the star pattern on the paper cover.
5. With the pointed end of the compass, make a hole through each star on the paper cover.
6. Place the flashlight inside the box. Darken the room and turn on the flashlight.
7. Turn the papered end of the box toward the ceiling. Move the flashlight back and forth in the box until a clear image of light spots appears on the ceiling.

Results An enlarged pattern of the holes in the paper are projected onto the ceiling.

Why? Light shining through the holes spreads out, producing larger circles of light on the ceiling. The stars projected on the ceiling are in the correct order as seen in the sky. The star pattern is the **constellation** (grouping of stars) called Draco.

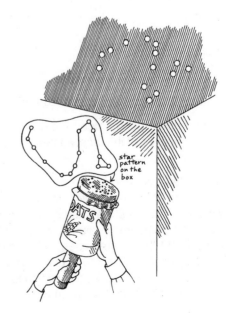

star pattern on the box

25. Sky Gazer

Purpose To demonstrate how a refracting telescope works.

Materials 2 magnifying lenses
sheet of notebook paper

Procedure
1. In a darkened room, close one eye and look at an open window through one of the magnifying lenses.
2. Move the lens back and forth slowly until the objects outside the window are clearly in focus.
3. Without moving the lens, place the paper between you and the lens.
4. Move the paper back and forth until a clear image appears on the sheet.
5. Replace the paper with the second lens.
6. Move the second lens back and forth to find the position where the image looks clear when looking through both lenses.

Results A small, inverted image of the objects outside the window is projected onto the paper. This image is larger when seen through both lenses.

Why? A **refracting telescope** has two lenses, an **objective lens** (the lens closer to the object being viewed) and an **eyepiece** (the lens closer to your eye). The two magnifying lenses in this activity represent the objective lens and eyepiece in a refracting telescope. The objective lens collects light from distant objects and brings it into focus in front of the eyepiece. This image can be projected onto a screen, such as the paper. When you look through the magnifying lens eyepiece or a real eyepiece in a telescope, you see the same image, but it is magnified.

26. Collector

Purpose To demonstrate the reflection of energy waves.

Materials television with a remote control
6-inch by 12-inch (15-cm by 30-cm) piece of aluminum foil
masking tape

Procedure
1. Use the remote control to change the channels on the television.
2. Cover the receiving eye on the television. Attach the foil with tape.
3. Try to change the channels using the remote control.

Results The remote control does not work when the aluminum foil is in front of the receiving eye on the television.

Why? The sun and other stars are constantly emitting energy in the form of waves. Radio waves, visible light, infrared waves, and others are examples of these energy waves. In this experiment, aluminum is used to **reflect** (bounce back) the infrared energy signals coming from the remote control. This metal also reflects radio waves and is used in making large bowl-shaped radio telescopes that reflect radio waves coming from distant stars. These reflected waves are directed toward a receiver that transmits them to a computer, and finally a recorded message is printed. A radio telescope in Arecibo, Puerto Rico, is the size of 13 football fields.

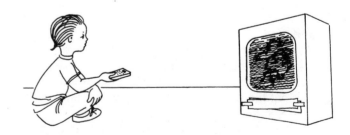

27. Focus

Purpose To determine why radio wave receivers are curved.

Materials scissors
index card
modeling clay
sheet of black construction paper
6-by-12-inch (15-by-30-cm) piece of aluminum foil
quart (liter) jar
flashlight

Procedure
1. Cut four 1-inch (2.5-cm) -high slits in the index card, about ¼ inch (.6 cm) wide and ¼ inch (.6 cm) apart.
2. Use clay to stand the card in the center of the paper.
3. Fold the aluminum foil in half lengthwise three times.
4. Mold the aluminum foil around the side of the jar to form a curved metal mirror.
5. Place the flashlight on one side of the card and the curved aluminum mirror on the opposite side.
6. In a darkened room, move the flashlight toward and away from the card until straight lines of light pass through the slits in the card.
7. Move the aluminum toward and away from the card until the clearest image is seen.

Results Lines of light reflected from the aluminum mirror leave the surface of the metal at an angle and cross at one point in front of the mirror.

Why? Light is reflected from the **concave** (crescent-shaped) mirror to a central focal point. Radio waves, like the light, can be reflected from concave surfaces to a point where a type of microphone is positioned to send the concentrated waves on to another receiver.

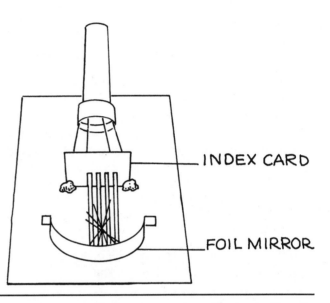

INDEX CARD

FOIL MIRROR

28. Around the World

Purpose To demonstrate how radio waves are sent around the earth via satellite.

Materials small coffee can
black construction paper
transparent tape
yardstick (meterstick)
scissors
modeling clay
flat mirror
flashlight

Procedure
1. Cover the outside of the can with the paper.
2. Tape a paper flap about 4 inches (10 cm) square to one side of the can.
3. Place the measuring stick in front of the can.
4. Use the clay to stand the mirror on top of the measuring stick near the can.
5. Darken the room. Place the flashlight at a slight angle to the can as shown.
6. Move the mirror and flashlight until light from the flashlight is projected onto the paper flap.

Results The mirror changes the direction of the light path.

Why? In this experiment the mirror represents a **satellite** above the earth (the can). Light from the flashlight represents radio waves and the paper is a receiver. The direction of the light is changed by reflecting it off a mirror. The direction of radio waves can also be changed by sending them to a satellite that sends them in another direction.

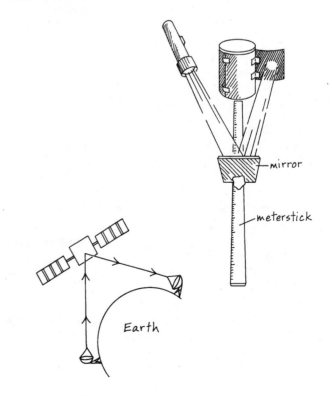

mirror

meterstick

Earth

29. Launcher

Purpose To demonstrate how satellites are launched into orbit around the earth.

Materials cardboard box
2 plastic rulers with grooves down the center
modeling clay
marble

Procedure
1. Place the cardboard box upside down on a table, with the edge of the box 10 inches (25 cm) from the edge of the table.
2. Lay one ruler on top of the box with 4 inches (10 cm) of the ruler extending over the edge of the box. This ruler will be called the launcher.
3. Hold the other ruler so that one end touches the launcher, with their grooves lined up, and the second end is supported with clay 2 inches (5 cm) above the box. The raised ruler represents power rockets.
4. Position a marble at the top of the raised ruler, and then release the marble. The marble represents a **satellite**.

Results The marble rolls down the rulers and off the end. Its path curves until it hits the floor.

Why? The table represents the earth. The top of the box is a position above the earth's surface. All **satellites** are raised to the desired height above the earth by booster rockets and then turned, so that with additional power rockets the satellite is launched parallel to the earth's surface. The marble satellite, like space satellites, moves in a curved path because **gravity** pulls it down as its launching speed pushes it forward.

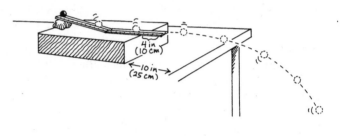

30. Escape

Purpose To demonstrate escape velocity.

Materials 12-by-4-inch (30-by-10-cm) strip of stiff paper
magnet, any size or shape
large plastic lid
transparent tape
modeling clay
box of steel air-gun shot, BBs

Procedure
1. Fold the paper lengthwise to form an M shape.
2. Place the magnet against the inside edge of the plastic lid.
3. Spread the M-shaped paper so that the center trough is widened, and tape one end to the edge of the magnet.
4. Use the clay to slightly elevate the unattached end of the paper trough.
5. Place one BB at the top of the trough and allow it to roll toward the magnet.
6. Raise the trough again and allow another BB to roll down. Continue to raise the trough until a rolling BB does not stick to the magnet.

Results The BBs roll down the trough and stick to the magnet when the trough is slightly raised. At a higher elevation, the BBs slow down when they touch the magnet, but roll past into the plastic lid.

Why? Raising the trough increases the **velocity**, or speed, of the BBs. The velocity of the BBs can be compared to the **escape velocity** (velocity needed to escape the earth's gravitational pull) of a rocket leaving the earth. The BBs are escaping the magnetic pull of the magnet, and the rocket is escaping the gravitational pull of the earth.

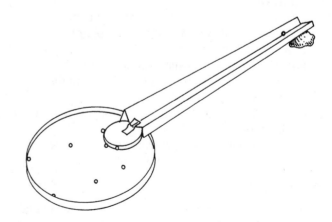

31. Blast Off

Purpose To demonstrate how rockets move in space.

Materials 9-inch (23-cm) balloon

Procedure
1. Inflate the balloon and hold the mouth of the balloon shut between your fingers.
2. Release the balloon and allow it to move freely.

Results The balloon moves around the room as it deflates.

Why? When the inflated balloon is closed, the air inside pushes equally in all directions. As the air leaves the balloon, the opening moves back and forth, like a rudder, which directs the balloon in an irregular path through the air. The balloon, like a rocket, moves because of *Newton's Third Law of Motion*, which states that for every action there is an equal and opposite reaction. In the case of the balloon, the rubber pushes on the air inside (action), forcing it out the opening. The air pushes on the balloon (reaction). The reaction force of the air pushes the balloon in the opposite direction of the action force. Like the balloon, spacecraft are able to move forward due to action-reaction forces. The engines of a rocket produce gases that are pushed out the exhaust (action), and the gas applies a force on the rocket (reaction). The reaction force pushes against the rocket, causing it to lift up.

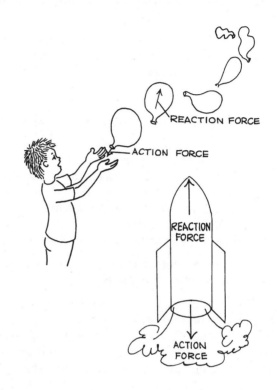

32. Pointer

Purpose To demonstrate how a gyroscope helps steer a spacecraft.

Materials large plastic lid from a can, such as a coffee can
18-inch (45-cm) piece of string
modeling clay
round toothpick
full-length mirror
adult helper

Procedure
1. Ask an adult to make a hole in the center of the plastic lid.
2. Thread the free end of the string through the hole and tie a knot on the underside.
3. Press a grape-sized piece of clay in the center of the lid on top of the knot. Stand the toothpick in the center of the clay.
4. Stand in front of the mirror and hold the string. Use your hand to start the lid spinning. This action also starts the lid swinging back and forth.
5. While looking in the mirror, continue swinging the lid back and forth. Observe the direction the toothpick points.

Results If the lid is spun fast enough, it spins horizontally, with the toothpick pointing straight down.

Why? The lid acts like a **gyroscope**, an instrument with a wheel or disk designed to spin around a central axis. As long as the lid spins rapidly, the direction of its spin axis, the toothpick, will not change. The resistance of a gyroscope's spin axis to change in direction makes it a useful device for aiming and steering spacecraft.

33. Spheres

Purpose   To simulate the release of a drop of liquid in space.

Materials   clear drinking glass   eyedropper
               tap water   liquid cooking oil
               rubbing alcohol

Procedure

CAUTION: Keep the alcohol away from your nose and mouth.

1. Fill the glass half full with water.
2. Tilt the glass and very slowly fill the glass with alcohol by pouring the alcohol down the inside of the glass. This will keep it from mixing with the water.
3. Add 4 to 5 drops of oil to the glass.
4. Observe the position of the oil and its shape.

Results   The oil falls through the alcohol and spheres of oil float between the alcohol and water layer.

Why?   The oil drops stay suspended between the layers of water and alcohol because the oil does not dissolve in either liquid. The oil is heavier than the alcohol but lighter than the water, and thus it falls through the alcohol and floats on the surface of the water. This pro-

duces the same results as releasing a drop of liquid in space. In both situations, the liquid drop forms a near-perfect **sphere** (ball shape).

34. Protector

Purpose   To determine how the materials in space suits help to regulate temperature.

Materials   2 drinking glasses
               rubber glove
               aluminum foil
               cotton handkerchief
               2 thermometers
               desk lamp

Procedure

1. Line one glass with the rubber glove, and cover the outside of the glass with aluminum foil.
2. Line the other glass with the handkerchief.
3. Place a thermometer in each glass and set both glasses about 12 inches (30 cm) from the lamp.
4. Observe the temperature on both thermometers after 5 minutes.

Results   The temperature is higher in the glass lined with the handkerchief.

Why?   **Insulators** are materials that help prevent temperature changes by slowing the transfer of heat energy. The rubber glove is a better insulator than the handkerchief. The aluminum foil helps keep the glass cooler by

reflecting light away from the glass. An astronaut's space suit must keep a constant temperature, and one way is to decrease the amount of heat transferred to and from the astronaut's body. Layers of insulating material, such as rubber and nylon, are used to make the suits, and an outer coating of aluminum is added to **reflect** the sun's rays.

35. Space Suit

Purpose To demonstrate how a space suit affects an astronaut's blood.

Materials sealed bottle of soda
timer

Procedure
1. Observe the liquid in the sealed bottle of soda for 10 to 15 seconds.
2. Open the bottle of soda.
3. Observe the liquid in the bottle for 10 to 15 seconds.

Results No bubbles are seen in the sealed bottle, but gas bubbles rise to the surface of the liquid in the open bottle.

Why? In the bottling process, high pressure is used to cause carbon dioxide gas to dissolve in the soda water. When the bottle is opened, the pressure decreases and a large amount of the gas rises to the surface of the liquid and escapes into the air. The pressure inside a space suit is great enough to keep dissolved gases in an astronaut's blood. If the space suit were punctured, the pressure inside the suit would decrease and bubbles of gas would come out of the blood as the bubbles in the soda did. Not only would gas bubbles escape the blood, but bubbles of gas inside the blood vessels could expand, causing the vessels to break.

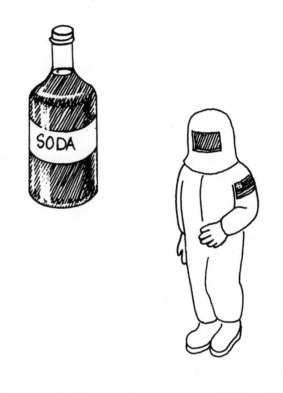

36. Fake

Purpose To demonstrate how artificial gravity can be produced.

Materials scissors
sheet of construction paper, any color
round cake pan
turntable
4 marbles

Procedure
1. Cut a circle of paper to fit inside the pan.
2. Center the pan on the turntable.
3. Place the marbles in the center of the pan.
4. Turn the turntable.

Results As the pan starts to spin, the marbles move forward until they hit the side of the pan.

Why? The movement of the pan starts the marbles moving. They move in a straight line until the side of the pan stops them. The marbles then press against the pan's side as long as the pan turns. In space, a turning space station would cause unattached objects inside to be pressed against the walls of the station just as the marbles press against the turning pan. A spinning space station would provide artificial **gravity** to allow astronauts to walk around and so that dropped objects fall "down," "down" being toward the outside rim of the turning craft. The most likely shape for a spinning space station would be a large wheel.

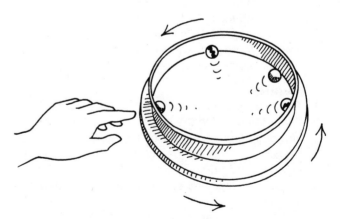

37. Weightlessness

Purpose To determine why astronauts orbiting the earth have a feeling of weightlessness.

Materials scissors
ruler
sheet of construction paper, any color
transparent tape
string
2-liter soda bottle

Procedure

1. Cut a 2-by-8-inch (5-by-20-cm) strip from the paper.
2. Fold the paper strip in half four times and tape the edges together.
3. Cut a 12-inch (30-cm) piece of string.
4. Tie one end of the string around the center of the folded paper.
5. Hold the free end of the string and insert the folded paper into the plastic soda bottle.
6. Pull up on the string until the bottle is about 2 inches (5 cm) above the table.
7. Release the string.
8. Observe the movement of the bottle and the folded paper.

Results When the string is released, the bottle and

the paper fall. The paper hangs at the top of the bottle until the bottle stops, and then the paper falls to the bottom of the bottle.

Why? Like the paper and bottle, astronauts and the spacecraft they are in fall at the same speed while **orbiting** the earth. As long as both are falling there is an apparent **weightlessness** (zero pull of **gravity**).

38. Taller

Purpose To determine how gravity affects height.

Materials scissors
2-liter soda bottle with cap
5 empty plastic thread spools
18-inch (45-cm) length of string
2-quart (2-liter) bowl
large pitcher of tap water
adult helper

Procedure

1. Ask an adult to remove the bottom from the soda bottle.
2. Place the string in the bottle with about 2 inches (5 cm) of string hanging out of the mouth of the bottle.
3. Secure the cap on the bottle, leaving part of the string hanging out.
4. Thread the free end of the string through the holes in the spools.
5. Set the bottle, cap side down, in the bowl.
6. Support the bottle in an upright position with your hand, and hold the upper end of the string with your free hand so that the spools stand straight. Notice the position of each spool.
7. Ask your helper to fill the plastic bottle with water while you continue to pull the string upward. Again, notice the position of each spool.

Results In the bottle full of water, the spools are separated and the top spool is higher in the bottle.

Why? The upward force by the water, called **buoyancy**, simulates a low-**gravity** environment. With less downward pull, the spools separate. Like the spools, the spine has a cord called the **spinal cord** (a large bundle of nerves that runs through the centers of the discs of the spine). Gravity pulls the discs down against each other. In space, the discs separate, and the spine gets longer because gravity is not pulling it down. Thus, astronauts are taller in space.

39. Overhead

Purpose To find the zenith of an object.

Materials 8-inch (20-cm) piece of string
12-inch (30-cm) ruler, with holes for a 3-ring binder
scissors
masking tape
pen

Procedure
1. Tie one end of the string to the hole in one end of the ruler.
2. Stick a 1-inch (2.5-cm)-long piece of tape on the end of the ruler that has the string.
3. Draw an arrow on the tape so that the arrow points toward the string.
4. Hold the end of the string and raise your arm so that the ruler hangs in front of you.
5. Observe the direction the arrow points.

NOTE: Keep the ruler for Experiment 40.

Results The arrow points up.

Why? **Gravity** pulls the hanging ruler toward the center of the earth. Thus, the bottom of the ruler points straight down and the top of the ruler points straight up.

Imagine a line going straight up from the top of the ruler and ending at a point in the sky directly above the ruler. That point is called the **zenith** (point in the sky directly above that object) of the ruler. Your zenith is different from that of the ruler. No two objects can have the same zenith at the same time because no two objects occupy the same space at the same time.

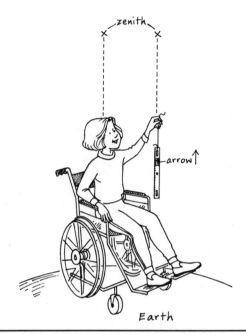

40. Below

Purpose To find the nadir of an object.

Materials scissors
masking tape
pen
ruler from Experiment 39

Procedure
1. Cut a piece of tape about 1 inch (2.5 cm) long.
2. Stick the tape to the end of the ruler opposite the previously taped end.
3. Draw an arrow on the tape so that the two arrows on the ruler point in opposite directions.
4. Hold the end of the string and raise your arm so the ruler hangs in front of you.
5. Observe the direction of both arrows.

Results One arrow points up and the other points down.

Why? **Gravity** pulls the bottom of the ruler toward the center of the earth; thus, the bottom arrow points toward the earth's center. Imagine a line going from the bottom arrow through the earth to a point in the sky on the opposite side of the earth. That point is called the nadir of the ruler. The **nadir** of an object is the point in the sky directly below that object on the other side of the earth, opposite the object's **zenith**.

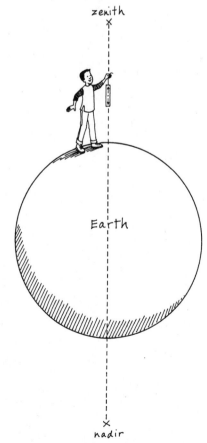

II
Biology

41. Too Big

Purpose To determine why dinosaur eggs were so small compared to the adult dinosaur.

Materials paper towel

Procedure
1. Hold the paper towel with both hands.
2. Stretch the paper towel slightly and place it against your mouth.
3. Blow through the paper towel. Make a mental note of the effort required to blow through the single layer.
4. Fold the paper towel in half and blow through the two layers. Compare the effort required to blow through the single and double layers.
5. Fold the paper towel in half again.
6. Try to blow through the four layers, and note how much effort it takes to blow through the added layers.

Results It becomes more difficult to blow through the paper towel as the number of layers increases.

Why? The shell of an egg, like the paper towel, permits air to flow through it if the layers are thin. But as the number of layers increases, it is more difficult for the air to pass through. In addition, the liquid inside the egg exerts pressure on the eggshell. Larger eggs require a thicker shell to hold back the increased pressure from the inside. Thicker shells not only would have been very difficult for the baby dinosaur to break out of, but also would have restricted the flow of air through the shell. Thus, the size and thickness of a dinosaur egg, like any egg, is limited.

42. Grinders

Purpose To determine how dinosaurs ate their food without grinding teeth.

Materials 20 green leaves from a large tree or bush (ask an adult to select the leaves)
2 resealable plastic bags
5 walnut-sized rocks

Procedure
1. Observe the shape of the leaves and then place 10 leaves in each plastic bag.
2. Add the rocks to one of the bags of leaves.
3. Hold the bag of leaves that does not contain the rocks between the palms of your hands.
4. Rub your hands together vigorously against the plastic bag 25 times. Observe the shape of the leaves.
5. Repeat step 4 with the other bag.

   NOTE: Do not rub so hard that you injure your hands.

Results The shape of the leaves in the bag that does not contain the rocks changes slightly or not at all. The leaves in the bag that contained the rocks are crushed.

Why? *Apatosaurus* and other dinosaurs with a similar body makeup probably did not chew their food, but swallowed it whole. Paleontologists have found large polished rocks near the rib bones of *Apatosaurus* fossils. The location of these rocks suggests that they were swallowed, just as modern chickens swallow gravel and use it to grind food inside their bodies. The food inside the dinosaur's body was pulverized by the rocks as the rocks moved around, just as the leaves were ground by the rocks in the bag.

43. Cooling Off

the index card, increases the flow of air across the skin. The moving air speeds the evaporation of the water, thus aiding in the cooling of the skin.

Purpose To determine how elephants use their ears to cool their bodies.

Materials paper towel
tap water
3-by-5-inch (7.5-by-12.5-cm) index card

Procedure

1. Wet the paper towel with water.
2. Rub the wet towel over the surface of your arm.
3. Hold the index card about 4 inches (10 cm) above your wet arm.
4. Quickly fan the index card back and forth about ten times. Observe any cooling effect on the skin.

Results The fanned wet skin feels cool.

Why? The cooling effect is due to the evaporation of the water from the skin. **Evaporation** occurs when a liquid absorbs enough heat energy to change from a liquid to a gas. The water takes energy away from the skin when it evaporates, causing the skin to cool. Elephants use their trunks to spray themselves with water; then they fan their bodies with their large ears. The fanning of their ears, like

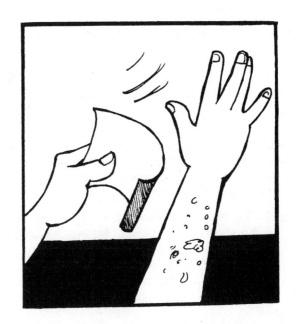

44. Fatty Insulators

Purpose To determine how the fat layer under the skin keeps an animal warm.

Materials two 7-ounce (210-ml) paper cups
shortening
2 thermometers
freezer
timer

Procedure

1. Fill one paper cup with shortening.
2. Insert one thermometer into the cup of shortening so that the bulb of the thermometer is in the center of the shortening.
3. Stand the other thermometer in the other paper cup.

   NOTE: Lay the cup on its side if the weight of the thermometer tends to topple the cup over.

4. Read and record the temperature shown on each thermometer. Then place the cups with their thermometers in the freezer and shut the door.
5. Read and record the temperature on each thermometer after 15 minutes.

Results In 15 minutes, the readings on the thermometer placed in the shortening changed very little, but the temperature inside the empty cup decreased rapidly.

Why? The shortening, like the fat layer under the skin of animals, acts as an **insulator** and, thus, restricts the heat flow away from the warm inner body to the frigid air outside the body. The heat inside the shortening, like that in an animal's body, is lost, but, because of the insulating fat, the loss is very slow. Food eaten by animals provides energy that continuously replaces the lost heat.

45. Feather Features

Purpose To study parts of a feather.

Materials feather
magnifying lens

NOTE: Purchase the feather at a craft store. Do not use a feather found on the ground.

Procedure
1. Gently pull apart one part of the feather as shown.
2. Study the surface of the feather with the lens and note the edges where the feather is pulled apart.

Results There are parallel ridges coming off both sides of the hard tubelike center of the feather. Where the feather is separated, there are hairlike structures along both separated edges.

Why? The feather is made up of a tubelike center called the **shaft**; the rest of the feather is called the **vane**. The vane is made up of **barbs** that look like strings coming off the shaft in parallel rows. Where two barbs are separated, tiny **barbules** grow from each of the barbs. On one side of a barb, the barbules are more hooked.

46. Zip

Purpose To demonstrate how birds repair their feathers.

Materials resealable plastic bag
feather

NOTE: Purchase the feather at a craft store. Do not use a feather found on the ground.

Procedure
1. Open the bag.
2. Put the open edges of the bag together and use your fingers to "zip" the bag closed.
3. Separate the vane on one side of the feather's shaft.
4. Use your fingers to push the separated section of the vane back together.
5. Move your fingers across the top and bottom of the feather in the same manner you "zipped" the plastic bag closed.

Results The bag and the feather both can be closed.

Why? Both the bag and the feather have edges that fit together. The **vane** of the feather is made of **barbs** with a rolled edge on one side and tiny hooks on the other side. These edges interlock when pressed together, just as the edges of the bag interlock. Birds press the barbs together with their beaks to keep their feathers smooth.

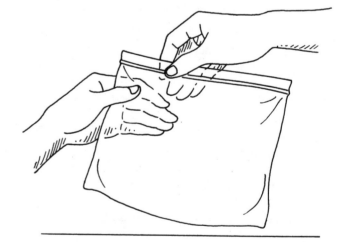

47. Sipper

Purpose To determine why hummingbirds have long, slender bills.

Materials tall, slender vase
tap water
drinking straw

Procedure
1. Fill the vase half full with water. Lower the straw into the vase.
2. With your finger over the end of the straw, lift the straw so that its open end is above the water.
3. Lift your finger from the straw's opening.

Results Water pours out of the straw into the vase.

Why? The straw is long enough to reach and remove the water in the vase. Hummingbirds have long, slender, hollow bills like the straw. The long, slender shape of their bills makes it easier for them to probe flowers for nectar.

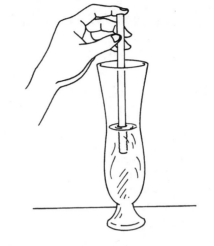

48. Night Crawlers

Purpose To determine how earthworms respond to light.

Materials scissors
shoe box with lid
flashlight
tape
notebook paper
tap water
paper towels
10 earthworms (purchase at a bait shop or dig your own)
timer

Procedure
1. Cut a hole slightly smaller than the flashlight's end in the end of the shoebox lid.
2. Tape a sheet of notebook paper to the lid so that it hangs about 1 inch (2.5 cm) from the floor of the shoe box, and about 4 inches (10 cm) from the end opposite the hole in the lid.
3. Place moistened paper towels in the bottom of the box.
4. Place the earthworms in the box under where the hole in the lid will be.
5. Position the flashlight over the hole and turn it on.
6. Leave the box undisturbed for 30 minutes, then open the lid and observe the position of the worms.
7. Return the worms to their natural surroundings—soil in a shady area outside.

Results The worms crawl away from the white light and under the paper partition where it is darker.

Why? Earthworms have no obvious sense organs such as eyes, but the worms respond to white light. Earthworms often surface at night and, therefore, are referred to as night crawlers.

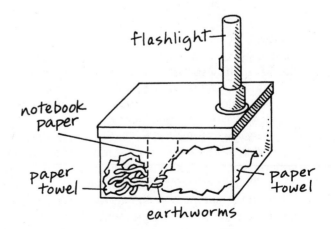

49. Earthworm Farm

Purpose To produce an environment suitable for earthworms.

Materials 2 cups (500 ml) soil
quart (liter) jar
tap water
1 cup (250 ml) peat moss
earthworms (purchase at a bait shop or dig your own)
apple peelings
dark construction paper
rubber band

Procedure

1. Pour the soil into the jar. Moisten the soil with water and keep it moist throughout the experiment.
2. Add the peat moss. Then put the worms into the jar.
3. Add the apple peelings.
4. Wrap the paper around the jar and secure with a rubber band. Place the jar in a shady, cool place.
5. Remove the paper and observe the jar every day for 7 days.
6. Return the worms to their natural surroundings— soil in a shady area outside.

Results The worms start wiggling and burrow into the soil. Tunnels are seen in the soil after a few days. The apple peelings disappear and pellets appear on the surface of the soil.

Why? An earthworm does not have jaws or teeth, but a muscle draws soil particles into its mouth. The worm extracts food from the soil, and the remaining part of the soil passes through the worm's body unchanged. Waste pellets called **casts** contain undigested soil and are deposited by the worm on the surface of the soil.

50. Cold Fish

Purpose To determine if temperature affects how a fish breathes.

Materials large-mouthed jar
aquarium with goldfish (or other small fish)
fish net
timer
large bowl
ice
tap water
thermometer
timer

Procedure

1. Fill the jar about three-fourths full with water from the aquarium. Use the net to transfer a fish to the jar.
2. Allow the fish 30 minutes to adjust to its new environment. Then, count the number of times the fish opens and closes its mouth in 1 minute.
3. Place the jar in the bowl. Fill the bowl half full with ice and then add enough water to fill the bowl. Do not add anything to the jar containing the fish.
4. Stand the thermometer inside the jar.
5. When the temperature in the jar reads 50 degrees Fahrenheit (10°C), count the number of times the fish opens and closes its mouth in 1 minute.

6. Pour the fish and the water in the jar back into the aquarium.

Results The fish breathes more often when the water temperature is warmer.

Why? Fish lose heat, thus losing energy, when the temperature around them is cold. Their body movements slow down to conserve energy. With slower body movements, the fish also breathes more slowly.

51. Chirper

Purpose To determine how temperature affects a cricket's chirp.

Materials cricket (purchase at a bait shop, pet store, or catch your own)
quart (liter) jar
old nylon stocking
rubber band
stopwatch

Procedure

NOTE: This activity should be performed on a warm day. Begin the activity in the early morning.

1. Place the cricket in the jar. Stretch the stocking over the mouth of the jar and secure it with the rubber band.
2. In the morning, the cooler part of the day, place the jar outside in the shade, then wait about 20 minutes.
3. Use the stopwatch to time yourself and count how many times the crickets chirps in 15 seconds. Count the chirps again in another 15-second period.
4. Repeat steps 2 and 3 during the hottest part of the day.
5. Release the cricket outside.

Results The cricket chirps more during the hottest part of the day.

Why? The temperature affects the activity of many animals. They are generally more sluggish when they are cool and more active when they are warm. Crickets are more active and chirp more when they are warm.

52. Distinctive

Purpose To determine how butterflies and moths differ.

Materials insect net
butterfly and moth (instructions for catching below)
2 large jars
2 old nylon knee-high stockings
2 rubber bands

Procedure
1. Use the insect net to catch a butterfly and a moth for this study.
2. Place the captured insects in separate jars. You can remove them from the net by holding the net over the jar and gently shaking out the insect.
3. Stretch a stocking over the mouth of each jar and secure with a rubber band.
4. View both insects through the glass and compare their differences.
5. Release the insects outside.

Results The insects differ in the shape of their antennae and abdomen and how they hold their wings.

Why? The butterfly holds its wings upward when resting, and the moth rests with its wings spread out. The butterfly's antennae are slender and clubbed at the end. Moths have all shapes and sizes of antennae, but their antennae are never clubbed and many are feathery. The body and abdomen of the moth is thicker and larger than the butterfly's.

butterfly   moth

53. Grasshopper

Purpose To determine the number of body parts of a grasshopper.

Materials insect net
     grasshopper (instructions for catching below)
     plastic vegetable bag
     magnifying lens

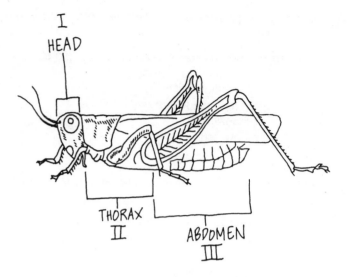

Procedure
1. It's better to use a dead grasshopper for this study, but if a dead grasshopper is not found, catch a live one with the net and place it in the plastic bag.
2. Move the live grasshopper to the corner of the bag so that it cannot move around.
3. Use the magnifying lens to study the body of the insect.
4. Release the live grasshopper outside.

Results The grasshopper's body has three main parts.

Why? Grasshoppers, like all insects, have three main body parts: the head, thorax, and abdomen.

54. BZZZZZ

Purpose To determine why insects make buzzing sounds.

Materials rubber band (large enough to fit tightly around the glass)
     juice glass
     index card

Procedure
1. Stretch the rubber band vertically around the glass, as shown in the diagram.
2. Pluck the rubber band with your finger.
3. Immediately touch the rubber band with a corner of the card.

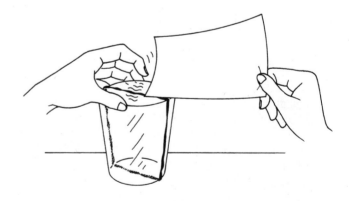

Results A buzzing sound is heard.

Why? **Sound** is produced when objects **vibrate** (move quickly back and forth). The **pitch** is the property of sound that makes it high or low. A high-pitched sound, such as the buzzing of the paper, is produced when an object vibrates many times per second. The same high-pitched buzzing sound is produced by the rapid back-and-forth movement of an insect's wings.

55. Geometric Designs

Purpose To determine if all spider webs have the same geometric design.

Materials spider webs
hairspray
baby powder
glue stick
dark construction paper
scissors
adult helper

Procedure

NOTE: The best time to find spider webs is in the early morning of a spring or summer day.

1. Pick out a suitable web for collecting and wait a few hours for any dew to dry. **CAUTION: Be sure the spider is gone before continuing.**
2. Spray the web with hairspray and immediately cover the web with powder.
3. Spray the paper with hairspray and push the sticky side against the web. Ask an adult to cut the web's support strands.
4. Allow the paper and web to dry.
5. Repeat steps 1 through 4 to collect as many different kinds of webs as possible. Compare the webs.

Results The web designs vary.

Why? Spiders of the same species do build webs of the same geometric design, but the design changes from one species to another.

56. Hidden

Purpose To demonstrate how color helps to protect an animal.

Materials scissors
ruler
2 sheets of construction paper (1 black and 1 orange)
2 sheets of newspaper (use sheets with print only—no pictures)
pencil
helper

Procedure

1. Cut two 3-by-5-inch (7.5-by-12.5-cm) rectangles from each sheet of construction paper and from one sheet of newspaper.
2. Stack the rectangles together. Draw the largest fish possible on the top piece.
3. Cut out the fish, making sure to cut through all 6 layers of paper. Do not allow your helper to see the fish before the experiment starts.
4. Lay the uncut sheet of newspaper on the floor at the feet of your helper.
5. Ask your helper to close his or her eyes while you scatter the paper fish on the newspaper. Be sure to lay the newspaper fish with the print-only side facing up.

6. When you say "Go," have your helper open his or her eyes, quickly look at the newspaper, count the paper fish that are laying on the newspaper, and then immediately raise his or her eyes from the newspaper.

Results Usually people see only the black and orange fish.

Why? The newspaper fish are an example of camouflage. **Camouflage** occurs when an animal's color blends into the color of its **environment** (the natural surroundings of an organism). Camouflage makes it difficult for an animal to be seen by a **predator** (an animal that lives by killing and eating other animals).

57. Decomposers

Purpose   To observe the effects of yeast on food decomposition.

Materials   butter knife
banana
2 resealable plastic bags
measuring spoon
dry yeast
marking pen

Procedure
1. Cut 2 slices from the banana.
2. Place one slice of banana inside each plastic bag.
3. Sprinkle ½ teaspoon (2.5 ml) of yeast on one of the banana slices.
4. Close both bags.
5. Label the bag containing the yeast Y.
6. Check each bag daily for one week. Observe and compare the amount and rate of decomposition of both slices.

Results   The banana covered with yeast shows the most and fastest decomposition.

Why?   Yeast is one of about 100,000 different kinds of organisms that make up the fungi group. **Fungi** must depend on other organisms for food. The yeast feeds on the banana, causing the banana to break into smaller parts. This breakdown is referred to as **decomposition**. Decomposers, like yeast, are an important part of our world because there is much dead material that must be broken into smaller parts and reused by plants and animals. The fertilizer used on plants and gardens has many decomposers working in it to make the material usable by the plants.

Before

After

58. Fuzz Balls

Purpose   To create an environment in which to grow penicillium.

Materials   2 oranges   2 cotton balls
2 lemons   tap water
bowl
2 bread sacks with twist ties

Procedure
1. Place the fruit in the bowl and expose it to the air for one day.
2. In each bread sack, place an orange, a lemon, and a cotton ball moistened with water.
3. Secure the ends of the sacks with a twist tie.
4. Place one sack in the refrigerator and the other in a warm, dark place.
5. Leave the sacks closed for two weeks and observe the fruit through the sacks as often as possible.
6. Discard the unopened bags.

Results   The fruit in the refrigerator has little or no change, but the other fruit has turned into blue-green fuzzy balls.

Why?   The green powdery growth on the outside of the fruit is penicillium. **Penicillium** is a mold from which penicillin, a medicine that kills germs, is made. Penicillium, like most molds, grows faster and in more abundance in moist warm places. This is why foods become more moldy in the summertime. Bread at room temperature molds more quickly than bread placed in a refrigerator. Cooling foods slows down the growth of mold, and freezing keeps foods fresh for much longer periods of time.

BAG FROM REFRIGERATOR

BAG LEFT OUT OF REFRIGERATOR

59. Mini-Organisms

Purpose To test the effect of preservatives on bacterial growth.

Materials chicken bouillon cube
1 cup (250 ml) warm tap water
3 small clear drinking glasses
1 teaspoon (5 ml) table salt
marking pen
masking tape
1 teaspoon (5 ml) white vinegar

Procedure
1. Dissolve the bouillon cube in the warm water.
2. Divide the solution equally between the 3 glasses.
3. Add the salt to one of the glasses. Use the marking pen and tape to label the glass Salt.
4. Add the vinegar to the second glass and label it Vinegar.
5. Label the third glass Control because it will not contain a preservative.
6. Place the three glasses in a warm place and observe after two days. Discard the contents of each glass.

Results The solution containing vinegar is the clearest. The control is the most cloudy.

Why? The cloudiness is due to the presence of large quantities of bacteria. The glasses containing the preservatives salt and vinegar are clearer than the control because the preservatives inhibit, or slow down, the growth of bacteria. Vinegar inhibits the bacterial growth better than salt does.

60. Passing Through

Purpose To symbolize how size affects movement of particles through a cell membrane.

Materials ½ cup (125 ml) table salt
½ cup (125 ml) pinto beans
quart (liter) jar, with lid
colander
large bowl
helper

Procedure
1. Pour the salt and beans into the jar.
2. Secure the lid and shake the jar back and forth several times to thoroughly mix the salt and beans.
3. Hold the colander over the bowl as your helper opens the jar and pours its contents into the colander.
4. Gently shake the colander up and down several times.
5. Observe the contents of the colander and bowl.

Results The salt falls through the holes in the colander and into the bowl. The beans remain in the colander.

Why? Cell membranes act like the colander, allowing passage of only those particles small enough to pass through the holes (in this case, salt). Particles larger than the holes (pinto beans) are prevented from passing through. Cells have a **semipermeable membrane**, which allows some materials to pass through but not others. Size is one selecting factor. Water passes through, but large particles do not.

61. Limp Spuds

Purpose To demonstrate osmosis.

Materials 1 tablespoon (15 ml) table salt
1 cup (230 ml) tap water
small bowl
spoon
potato
timer
adult helper

Procedure

1. Add the salt and water to the bowl. Stir.
2. Have an adult cut 3 potato slices, about ¼ inch (6 mm) thick.
3. Place the potato slices in the bowl of salt water.
4. After 15 minutes, pick up the potato slices one at a time. Test their hardness by trying to bend the slices.

Results The slices are very limp and bend easily.

Why? **Osmosis** is the movement of water through a **semipermeable membrane**. Water always moves through a membrane toward the side containing the most dissolved material, such as salt. The potato slices soaked in salt water feel limp because they have lost some of the original water inside their cells. The water from inside each potato slice moves out of the potato through cell membranes and into the bowl of salt water.

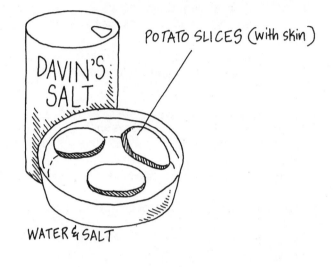

POTATO SLICES (with skin)

DAVIN'S SALT

WATER & SALT

62. Transporter

Purpose To observe the movement of water through a leaf.

Materials juice glass
tap water
red food coloring
scissors
large tree leaf, such as oak
adult helper

Procedure

1. Fill the glass about one-fourth full with water.
2. Add enough food coloring to make the water a deep red color.
3. Ask an adult to cut off the end of the leaf's stem.
4. Stand the leaf in the glass of colored water
5. Observe the color of the leaf for 2 days.

Results The red color slowly moves through the leaf, first following the pattern of the leaf veins and then spreading throughout the leaf.

Why? The plant leaf and stem contain tubes called **xylem**. These tubes transport water from the roots to other parts of the plant. In this activity, the colored water from the glass moves through these tubes to all parts of the leaf.

63. Sweetened Leaves

Purpose To demonstrate how nutrients in the soil are transported to the leaves of plants.

Materials masking tape
marking pen
3 glasses
2 tablespoons (30 ml) sugar
tap water
spoon
3 fresh stalks of celery with leaves

Procedure

NOTE: Never taste anything in a laboratory setting unless you are sure that it does not contain harmful chemicals or materials.

1. Use the tape and marking pen to label the glasses 1, 2, and 3, respectively.
2. Add 1 tablespoon (15 ml) of sugar to glasses 2 and 3.
3. Fill glasses 1 and 2 half full with water. Stir the water in glass 2 to dissolve the sugar.
4. Stand a stalk of celery in each glass.
5. Place the glasses in a refrigerator.
6. Wait 48 hours, then taste the leaves from each celery stalk.

Results The leaves on the celery standing in glass 2 taste sweet and those of the celery in the other glasses do not.

Why? As it dissolves sugar, water dissolves nutrients in soil and moves into the plant through the roots. From the roots, this liquid moves through **xylem** tubes to the leaves and other parts of the plant.

64. Trickery

Purpose To make a spring plant flower in the winter.

Materials 4 round toothpicks
flower bulb, such as hyacinth or paper whites
quart (liter) jar
tap water
sheet of dark construction paper
transparent tape
adult helper

Procedure

NOTE: This activity should be performed in the winter.

1. Ask an adult to insert toothpicks horizontally into the bulb on all four sides.
2. Fill the jar nearly full with water.
3. Wrap the paper around the jar and secure with tape.
4. Place the bulb in the jar so that the toothpicks rest on the mouth of the jar and the bottom of the bulb just touches the top of the water. Remove some of the water if it rises above the bottom of the bulb.
5. Place the bulb and jar in a warm, lighted area, such as near a window, for 2 to 4 weeks.

Results The bulb develops roots, stems, and a flower.

Why? Bulbs normally sprout in the spring when the soil becomes warm. Plants do not think and cannot really be tricked, but when you put the bulb in a warm place, the bulb behaves as if it were spring and starts to grow. The dark paper protects the roots from light like the soil does when plants are grown in the ground.

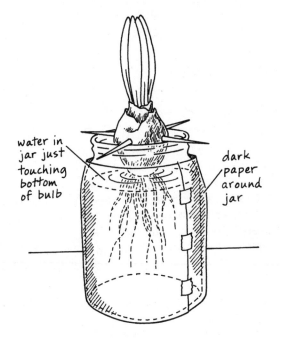

water in jar just touching bottom of bulb

dark paper around jar

65. Helicopter Seeds

Purpose To demonstrate the movement of fallen maple seeds.

Materials pencil   scissors
ruler   small paper clip
sheet of typing paper

Procedure
1. Draw a triangle with 4-inch (10-cm) sides on the paper.
2. Cut a 1-inch (2.5-cm) slit in the center of one side, perpendicular to the side.
3. Draw a fold line at the end of the slit, perpendicular to the slit and parallel to the side in which you cut the slit.
4. Label the area left of the slit with an A, label the area right of the slit with a B, and write Body on the lower part, as shown in the diagram.
5. Fold along the fold line so that area A points away from you and area B points toward you.
6. Place the paper clip across the pointed tip of the paper.
7. Hold the paper as high as possible and drop it.

Results The paper twirls around.

Why? The paper is shaped so that as it drops, it twirls like the blades of a helicopter. Maple seeds have a similar shape and also twirl as they fall. Both the paper and the maple seeds twirl because some of the air hitting the undersides of the blades is directed toward the body. Since the blades are on different sides, this air flow pushes the body from different directions, causing it to spin around.

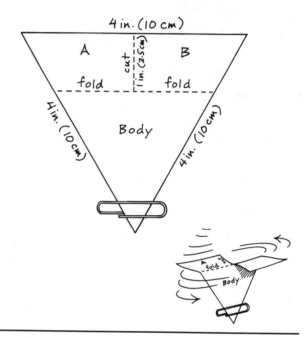

66. Stuck

Purpose To determine how cocklebur seeds and hook-and-loop fasteners like Velcro are alike.

Materials 1-by-6-inch (2.5-by-15-cm) pair of hook-and-loop fastener strips (purchase at a fabric store)
magnifying lens

Procedure
1. Use the magnifying lens to study the "sticky" surfaces of the hook-and-loop strips.

Results One surface is covered with rows of hooks, and the other is covered with a mass of threadlike loops.

Why? Hook-and-loop fasteners are designed after the cocklebur seed, which is covered with hooks that get stuck in the fur of animals when they brush against the seed. The fastener strips' hooks and loops are usually made from a blend of polyester and nylon. Like cocklebur seeds, the hooks on the surface of one fastener strip catch in the loops on the surface of the other strip. The joined hooks and loops hold the strips tightly together.

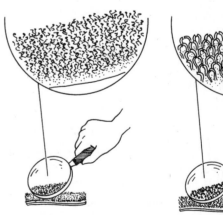

67. Grow a Bean

Purpose To determine if the way seeds are planted affects the direction of root growth.

Materials paper towels
clear drinking glass
masking tape
marking pen
4 pole snap beans, such as Kentucky
    Wonder
tap water

Procedure
1. Fold one paper towel and line the inside of the glass with it. Wad several paper towels and stuff them into the glass to hold the paper lining tightly against the glass.
2. Place a strip of tape around the outside of the glass.
3. On four sides of the glass, mark the tape with an arrow to indicate up, down, left, and right.
4. Place one bean between the glass and the paper towel lining under each arrow. Point the bean's concave side in the direction indicated by the arrow.
5. Moisten the paper towels in the glass with water. The paper should be moist, not dripping wet.
6. Keep the paper moist and observe for 5 to 7 days.

NOTE: Keep the glass of beans for Experiment 67.

Results No matter in which direction the bean is planted, the roots grow downward.

Why? Plants contain **auxin**, a chemical that changes the speed of plant growth. **Gravity** causes the auxin to collect in the lower part of the plant. Root cells grow faster on the side where there is a smaller amount of auxin, causing this section to bend downward. The result is that auxin causes roots to grow down.

68. Winders

Purpose To determine the direction of winding plants.

Materials masking tape
4 pencils
glass of growing beans from Experiment
    66
tap water

Procedure
1. Tape one pencil vertically to the outside of the glass in front of each plant. Have as much of the pencil as possible sticking up above the glass.
2. Allow the plant to stand for 2 weeks or longer. Be sure to keep the paper toweling in the glass moist with water.

Results The bean stems wind around the pencils.

Why? The winding occurs because the part of the stem that is being touched does not grow as fast as the outside. As the outside of the stem increases in size, it forces the stem to wrap around whatever object it touches.

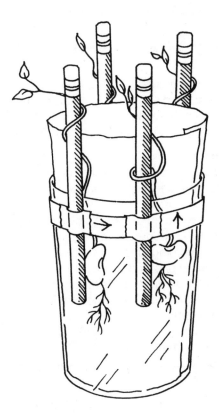

69. Growth Rate

Purpose To determine how shade affects stem growth in plants.

Materials ruler
4 green onions
scissors
2 glasses
potting soil
tap water
pencil
adult helper

Procedure
1. Measure about 6 inches (15 cm) from the root of each green onion and ask an adult to cut off the stems.
2. Fill the glasses with soil and moisten the soil with water.
3. In the soil of each glass, use the pencil to make 2 holes about 2 inches (5 cm) deep near the side of the glass.
4. Plant one onion in each hole.
5. Place one glass near a window so that it receives sunlight and place the other glass in a shady part of the room.
6. Each day for 14 days, mark each stem just above the outer skin covering, as shown in the diagram.

Results The stems on the onions placed in the shade are longer than those placed in the sun.

Why? The lack of sunlight triggers growth in the onion stems as in all plant stems. This growth increases a plant's chances of growing out from under the shade. If the plant does not reach sufficient sunlight, however, it will eventually die.

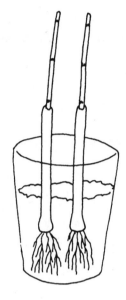

70. Flower Maze

Purpose To demonstrate that plants grow toward light.

Materials paper cup
potting soil
3 pinto beans
tap water
scissors
cardboard
shoe box with a lid
masking tape

Procedure
1. Fill the cup with soil and plant the beans in the soil.
2. Moisten the soil and allow the beans to sprout (about 5 to 7 days).
3. Cut two cardboard pieces to fit inside the shoe box.
4. Secure the cardboard with tape to form a maze, as shown in the diagram.
5. Cut a hole at one end of the lid.
6. Place the bean plant inside the shoe box at one end.
7. Secure the box lid with the hole on the opposite end from the plant.
8. Open the lid daily to observe the plant's growth. Water the soil when needed.
9. Continue to observe until the plant grows out the hole in the lid.

Results The plant winds around the obstacles and out the hole in the lid.

Why? The plant grows toward the light. This growth of a plant in response to light is called **phototropism**. A buildup of **auxin** occurs on the dark side of the stem. Auxin causes stem cells to grow longer on the dark side, which forces the stem to bend toward light.

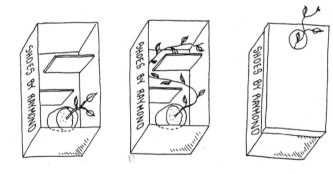

71. Growing Season

Purpose To demonstrate the effect of temperature on seed growth.

Materials 2 drinking glasses / 8 pinto beans / paper towels / tap water

Procedure
1. Prepare both glasses as follows:
   a. Fold one paper towel and line the inside of the glass with it.
   b. Wad several paper towels and stuff them into the glass to hold the paper lining against the glass.
   c. Place four beans between the glass and the paper towel lining. Evenly space the beans around the center of the glass.
2. Moisten the paper towels in the glasses with water. The paper should be moist but not dripping wet.
3. Place one glass in the refrigerator and keep the other at normal room temperature.
4. Keep the paper in both glasses moist and observe for 7 or more days.

Results The beans at room temperature have started to grow, but the ones in the refrigerator are unchanged.

Why? Seeds need a specific temperature to grow, and pinto beans require warmth. Very few seeds sprout dur-

ing the colder months. Most are **dormant** (inactive) during the cold parts of the year and start to grow when the ground warms.

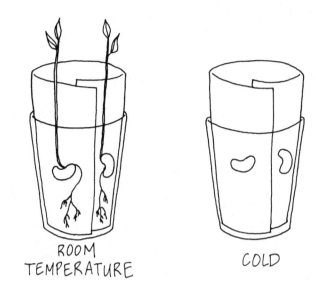

ROOM TEMPERATURE   COLD

72. Pictures from Sound

Purpose To show that the mind can change sound messages into mental pictures.

Materials scissors
poster board
2 cardboard school boxes
marking pen
masking tape
2 marbles
helper

Procedure
1. Prepare two boxes without your helper seeing their contents.
2. Cut 2 strips from the poster board. One must fit diagonally across the inside of a school box and the other must fit perpendicularly across the inside of the box. Be sure the lid of the box will close when these strips are in position.
3. Label one box 1 and tape the paper strip diagonally across. Add one marble and tape the box closed.
4. Label the other box 2 and tape the paper strip perpendicularly across the box. Add one marble and tape the box closed.
5. Ask your helper to rotate each box back and forth

and determine the shape of the open space inside each box from the sounds heard.

Results The sound of the rolling marble allows your helper to determine the inside structure of each box.

Why? As the marble moves around, your helper makes mental notes about the length of time before the marble hits something. When enough information is put together, your helper can form a mental picture of the inside of each box.

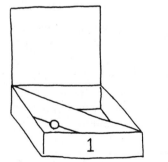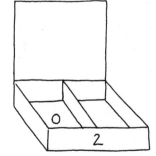

73. Concentration

Purpose To test your power of concentration.

Materials chair

Procedure
1. Sit in the chair with your feet on the floor.
2. Use your right foot to trace a clockwise pattern on the floor.
3. Keep your foot going in a circle while you move your right hand around in a clockwise pattern in front of your body.
4. Continue tracing the circular pattern with your foot, but change the hand pattern to an up-and-down motion.

Results It is easy for the foot and hand to perform the same pattern of movement, but difficult to move them simultaneously in two different patterns.

Why? When the patterns for hand and foot are the same, repetitive movement is easy. Up-and-down or circular patterns are easily done, but only when one pattern at a time is being processed by the brain. It takes much concentration and practice to successfully accomplish both patterns simultaneously.

74. In the Way

Purpose To demonstrate the body's automatic balance responses.

Materials wall

Procedure
1. Stand with your feet about 12 inches (30 cm) apart, and with your right foot and right shoulder against the wall.
2. Try to bend your left knee so that your left foot is lifted about 4 inches (10 cm) above the floor.

Results You start to fall over when you raise your foot.

Why? Raising the left foot causes the body's **center of gravity** to extend past the body's supportive foundation—the foot on the floor. The body automatically leans slightly to the right to redistribute the body's weight and again place its center of gravity over the supportive foot. When standing next to the wall, the body is prevented from leaning to the right, so you cannot balance with your foot raised.

75. Blinking

Purpose To determine if blinking is an involuntary action.

Materials helper who wears glasses or lightly tinted
sunglasses
cotton ball

NOTE: If sunglasses are used, they must be lightly tinted so that you can easily see your helper's eyes through them.

Procedure

CAUTION: Do not substitute materials without adult approval. It could be dangerous to throw anything other than a cotton ball.

1. Have your helper wear his or her glasses.
2. Stand about 1 yard (1 m) away from your helper.
3. Without letting your helper know it's coming, throw a cotton ball directly at your helper's face. The glasses will keep the cotton ball from hitting your helper in the eyes.

Results Your helper will blink, and possibly jerk or raise a hand, to protect his or her eyes.

Why? The sudden unexpected approach of the cotton ball causes your helper's eyes to blink. Blinking is a reflex action. Like other reflex actions, it is not controlled by thinking about it. The involuntary movement of the eyelids, head, and hand happens because nerve cells in the eyes send messages to nerve cells in the brain and **spinal cord**. The instructions are then quickly passed on to the muscles, resulting in the protective movements of blinking, jerking the head, and raising the hand in front of the face.

76. Numb

Purpose To demonstrate how the brain interprets messages from sensory receptors in the skin.

Materials pencil

Procedure

1. Use your index finger and thumb of your right hand to rub the upper- and undersides of the index finger of your left hand.
2. Hold the pencil in your left hand against the underside of the index finger on that hand.
3. Rub the upper side of your left index finger and the pencil at the same time.

Results When the pencil is held against the finger and both are rubbed, it feels as if part of your finger is numb.

Why? When you rub your finger, **mechanoreceptors** (cells that are stimulated by pressure, touch, or sound) on both sides of the touched finger send messages to the brain. Mechanoreceptors on the finger and thumb of the hand doing the rubbing are also sending messages. These messages are analyzed by the brain, which sends an output message that results in the sensation that you are rubbing both sides of your finger. When the pencil is rubbed instead of the finger's underside, a message is missing. The brain interprets the missing information to mean that the finger is numb on one side. The brain takes in and puts out information based on what the sensory receptors tell it. Even though you know better, the output message is that your finger is numb.

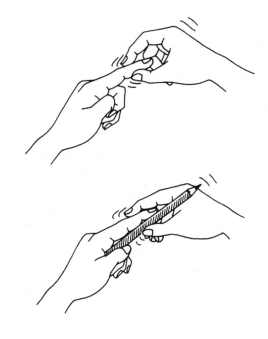

77. Open and Close

Purpose To demonstrate the ability of the eye's pupil to change size.

Materials penlight
helper

Procedure
1. Ask your helper to sit in a very dimly lighted room with both eyes open.
2. After 2 to 3 minutes, observe the size of the pupils in both eyes.
3. Hold the penlight close to, but not touching, the side of your helper's face. Slowly move the penlight so that the beam of light moves across the side of the face and shines directly into the pupil of one eye. Immediately turn off the penlight.

   CAUTION: Do not shine the light into your helper's eye for more than 1 second.

4. Repeat the previous step with the opposite eye.
5. Compare the size of the pupils before and after shining the light into the eyes.

Results The pupils are much larger before shining a light into the eyes.

Why? The **iris** (colored muscular circle in the front of the eye) controls the amount of light entering the eye by making the dotlike opening in its center, the **pupil**, larger or smaller. In dim light, the pupil **dilates** (gets bigger), allowing more light to enter the eye. In bright light, the pupil **contracts** (gets smaller) to protect the inside of the eye from excessive light.

78. Muscle Power

Purpose To locate the muscle pair in the upper arm.

Materials chair
helper

Procedure
1. Ask your helper to sit in the chair next to a heavy table.
2. Instruct your helper to place one hand, palm up, under the table's edge and push up carefully with medium pressure.
3. While pressure is being applied to the table, feel the front and back of your helper's upper arm.
4. Next, ask your helper to place his or her hand, palm down, on top of the table and to press down.
5. Again, feel the same parts of your helper's upper arm.

Results The muscle in front of the arm feels harder than the muscle in the back of the arm when the hand is pushing up on the table. The muscle in the back of the arm feels harder when the hand is pressing down on the table.

Why? Even though the **joint** (place where bones meet) in the arm—the elbow—is not being bent and straightened, the muscle pair in the upper arm that causes these movements is identified in this activity. Pushing up on the table causes the **flexor muscle** (muscle that bends a joint) in the front of the arm to **contract** and harden. Pushing down on the table causes the **extensor muscle** (muscle that straightens a joint) in the back of the arm to contract and harden.

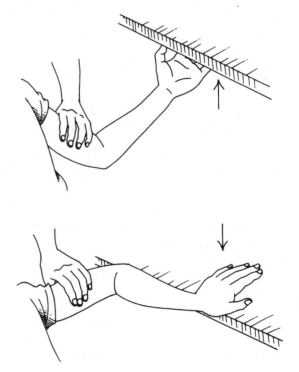

79. Stronger

Purpose To determine how sniffing affects the intensity of smells.

Materials vanilla extract   baby food jar
2 cotton balls   timer

Procedure
1. Place a few drops of the vanilla on one of the cotton balls.
2. Drop the moistened cotton ball into the jar.
3. Hold the opening of the jar under, but not touching, your nose.
4. Breathe normally for one or two breaths and note the strength of the smell of the vanilla.
5. Discard the cotton ball in the jar.
6. Wait 5 minutes, then repeat steps 1 and 2 with the other cotton ball, again holding the opening of the jar under, but not touching, your nose.
7. Take a good sniff by inhaling deeply.

Results The smell of the vanilla is stronger when you take a good sniff than when you breathe normally.

Why? In normal breathing, some of the air carrying the vanilla **molecules** (smallest particles of a substance) fills the nasal cavity but most of the air passes through the nasal cavity and into the back of the throat. When you take a good sniff, currents of air are drawn upward, flowing over the **chemoreceptors** (cells that are stimulated by smell or taste) located high up at the back of your nose. Sniffing also brings in more air containing the vanilla molecules.

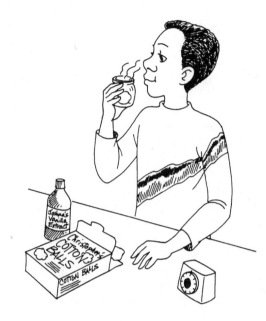

---

80. Hot or Cold?

Purpose To demonstrate that sensations of cold or hot can be deceiving.

Materials three 2-quart (2-liter) bowls
cold and warm tap water
5 ice cubes
spoon
thermometer

Procedure
1. Fill two of the bowls three-fourths full with cold tap water. Allow one bowl to stand for 5 minutes to reach room temperature. This will be the medium water.
2. Add the ice cubes to the second bowl. Stir until the ice cubes are about half melted. This will be the cold water.
3. Fill the third bowl three-fourths full with warm tap water. This will be the warm water. Use the thermometer to make sure it is about 113 degrees Fahrenheit (45°C).

   CAUTION: If hotter, add cold water, stir, and check the temperature before proceeding.

4. Place the bowls on a table with the cold water on your right, the medium water in the middle, and the warm water on your left.

5. Put your right hand in the cold water and your left hand in the warm water. After 20 seconds, remove your hands from the outer bowls and put both hands in the center bowl.

Results The same water feels warm to your right hand but cold to your left hand.

Why? Heat tends to flow from an object with a higher temperature to an object with a lower temperature. The medium water feels warm to your right hand because it had been soaking in icy water. The heat energy flowed from the warm water to your skin. The skin of your left hand was warmer than the medium water. Thus, the energy flow was away from the skin, making the medium water feel cold to your left hand.

cold   medium   warm

81. Gripper

Purpose To determine how the ridges on fingertips affect the ability to pick up objects.

Materials dishwashing gloves
assortment of small coins

Procedure
1. Put one glove on the hand you write with.
2. Spread the coins out on a table.
3. Pick up each coin one at a time with the hand covered with the rubber glove. Place each coin back on the table before lifting the next coin.
4. Make note of the ease or difficulty in lifting each coin from the table's surface.
5. Note the texture of the fingers of the gloves.
6. Remove the glove from your hand.
7. Turn the glove that does not fit your writing hand inside out.
8. Put the inside-out glove on your writing hand.
9. Again, pick each coin up one at a time with the hand covered with the rubber glove. Place each coin back on the table before lifting the next coin.
10. Make note of the ease or difficulty in lifting each coin from the table's surface.
11. Again, note the texture of the fingers of the glove.

Results The coins are easily picked up when the glove is right side out, but are difficult or impossible to pick up when the glove is inside out.

Why? The fingertips are rough when the glove is on properly and smooth when the glove is inside out. The textured tips of the glove act like the ridged skin on the tips of your fingers, the ridges that cause fingerprints. The ridges in the rubber, as well as in your skin, increase friction and allow you to pick up objects more easily. **Friction** is the resistance to motion between two surfaces that are touching each other. Without the ridges on your fingertips, your fingers would tend to slide over objects, making it difficult to pick them up, just as it was difficult with the smooth tips of the inside-out glove.

82. Hummer

Purpose To determine how you make sounds.

Procedure
1. Hum a tune with your mouth open.
2. Continue to hum, but close your mouth.
3. Pinch your nose closed with your fingers and hum with your mouth open.
4. Close your mouth, hum a tune, and pinch your nose closed again.

Results You can hum as long as your mouth and/or your nose is open, but if both are closed, you cannot hum.

Why? When you hum or make any other **sounds**, air passes between the vocal cords in your throat and causes them to **vibrate**. When your mouth and nose are closed, the air flow stops. Thus, the vibrations stop and the sound stops along with them.

III
Chemistry

83. Building Blocks

Purpose   To build a model of a lithium atom.

Materials   scissors
ruler
stiff wire
red, green, and yellow modeling clay
string

Procedure

1. Cut two pieces of wire, one 12 inches (30 cm) long and the other 18 inches (45 cm) long.
2. Bend and shape the wires into two circles as shown. Use clay to support the circles.
3. Cut a 6-inch (15-cm) piece of string and tie the string to the top of the inner wire circle.
4. Mold small balls from the clay. Make three red balls, three yellow, and four green.
5. Press two of the red balls onto the inner circle of wire, one on each side.
6. Press the third ball of red clay onto the outer circle of wire, on the right side.
7. Press the yellow clay balls and the green clay balls together around the string so that they are hanging at the center of the circle. Trim away any excess string.

Results   You have made a three-dimensional model of a lithium atom, showing the position of the atom's electrons (red), protons (yellow), and neutrons (green).

Why?   **Atoms** are the smallest building blocks of **matter** (any substance that takes up space and has weight). Atoms are made of smaller particles called **protons** (which have a positive charge), **electrons** (which have a negative charge), and **neutrons** (which are neutral, having neither a positive nor a negative charge). A lithium atom has three protons and four neutrons in its **nucleus** (the central part of the atom) and three electrons outside the nucleus.

84. Bonded

Purpose   To make a model of the physical structure of methane.

Materials   4 toothpicks
1 large black gumdrop
4 small white gumdrops

Procedure

1. Stick the toothpicks into the black gumdrop. Space the toothpicks so that they are an equal distance from each other.
2. Place a white gumdrop on the end of each toothpick.

Results   You have made a three-dimensional model of a methane molecule.

Why?   Methane is a hydrocarbon **molecule**. **Hydrocarbon** molecules are composed of carbon and hydrogen **atoms**. Each carbon atom in a hydrocarbon molecule has four **bonds** (connections between atoms) that are equally spaced, and each hydrogen atom has one bond. Methane is the simplest hydrocarbon molecule. In your methane model, the single black gumdrop represents one carbon atom bonded (attached) to four hydrogen atoms represented by the white gumdrops. The chemical formula used to represent methane is CH_4. The formula, like the model you made, shows that the methane molecule has one carbon atom and four hydrogen atoms.

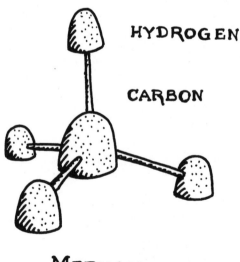

HYDROGEN

CARBON

METHANE

85. On the Move

Purpose To determine if water molecules are in constant motion.

Materials measuring cup
tap water
¼ teaspoon (1 ml) salt
green food coloring
spoon
clear juice glass
index card

Procedure
1. Measure ¼ cup (60 ml) water into the measuring cup. Add salt and 5 drops of coloring. Stir.
2. Fill the glass one-fourth full with water.
3. Tilt the glass, and slowly pour the green salt water down the side.
4. Cover the top of the glass with the index card, and place the glass where it will not be disturbed.
5. Observe the glass as often as possible for 2 days.

Results At first, the green salty water settles to the bottom of the glass and the clear water floats on top. After 2 days, all of the liquid in the glass is green.

Why? The green salty water sinks under the clear water because the salt water is heavier than the clear water. With time, the liquids mix together. This mixing is caused by the constant motion of the water **molecules.** The mixing of molecules because of molecular motion is called **diffusion.**

86. Spacey

Purpose To determine if water molecules in liquid water fit tightly together.

Materials clear drinking glass
plate
tap water
paper towel
1-teaspoon (5-ml) measuring spoon
table salt

Procedure
1. Place the glass on the plate.
2. Fill the glass to the brim with water. Stop adding the water when a tiny stream of water starts to flow over the side of the glass. (If you look sideways at the surface of the water, you can see it "bulging" over the top of the glass.)
3. Without moving the glass or plate, carefully blot up the water in the plate with the paper towel.
4. Fill the measuring spoon with salt.
5. Very slowly sprinkle salt crystals into the glass of water. If you use the entire spoonful, fill the spoon again.
6. Continue to add salt until water spills over the top of the glass.

Results The amount of salt that can be added before the water spills depends on the size of the glass.

Why? The grains of salt are made of tiny **molecules.** These molecules break away from each other and freely move around in the water. The water molecules in liquid water are connected in such a way that small empty pockets are formed. Separate salt molecules are small enough to easily fit into the spaces between the connected water molecules.

87. Beads

Purpose To determine why water forms beads on certain surfaces.

Materials saucer
baby powder
red, blue, or green food coloring in a
    dropper bottle

Procedure
1. Cover the saucer with a thin layer of powder.
2. Place several drops of food coloring on the powder layer.

NOTE: *Keep the results of this activity for Experiment 88.*

Results The food coloring forms colored balls on the powder's surface.

Why? Food coloring is colored water. Water forms beads on certain surfaces because of the surface tension of liquids. **Surface tension** is the tendency of **molecules** to cling together at the surface of a liquid to form a skinlike film. The surface molecules tend to pull inward on each other to form a **sphere**. This occurs when water molecules are more attracted to each other than to the surface they touch.

88. Spreader

Purpose To demonstrate the decrease of water's surface tension.

Materials dishwashing liquid
saucer
toothpick
saucer with beads of colored water from
    Experiment 87

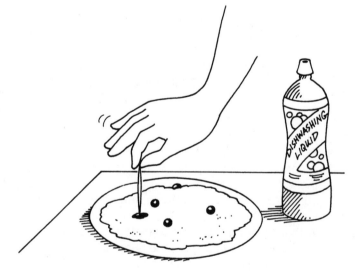

Procedure
1. Pour a drop of dishwashing liquid on the saucer.
2. Dip the end of the toothpick into the drop of dishwashing liquid.
3. Touch the wet end of the toothpick to several of the colored beads on the powder.

Results The beads break open and spread out.

Why? The detergent **molecules** in the dishwashing liquid move between the water molecules that make up the surface of the colored beads. The presence of the detergent molecules decreases the strong attractive forces between the water molecules. Thus, the **surface tension** of the water decreases, and the beads break apart.

89. Dipper

Purpose To determine when and why the surface of water dips in the center.

Materials paper hole-punch
sheet of typing paper
small glass with no more than a 2-inch (5-cm) diameter (a candle holder or an egg holder will work)
tap water

Procedure
1. Use the hole-punch to cut 3 or 4 circles from the paper.
2. Fill the glass about three-quarters full with water.
3. When the water is calm, place the paper circles on the surface in the center.

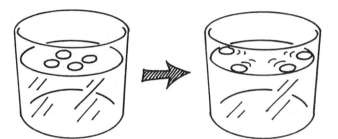

Results After a few seconds the paper moves to the side.

Why? In the partially filled glass, surface water **molecules** are more attracted to the sides of the glass than to each other. This attraction causes the surface water molecules to be pulled toward the glass, carrying the lightweight paper circles with them. The water rises up the sides of the glass, causing the surface of the water to dip in the center.

90. Bulge

Purpose To determine when and why the surface of water bulges in the center.

Materials paper hole-punch
sheet of typing paper
small glass with no more than a 2-inch (5-cm) diameter (a candle holder or an egg holder will work)
saucer
tap water
toothpick

Procedure
1. Use the hole-punch to cut 3 or 4 circles from the paper.
2. Place the glass in the saucer.
3. Fill the glass to overflowing with water. The surface of the water should bulge above the sides of the glass.
4. When the water is calm, place the paper circles on the surface of the water in the center.
5. Use the toothpick to move the circles toward the edge carefully, then release them. Be sure that you do not force the water over the edge of the glass.
6. Repeat the previous step.

Results The paper circles continue to move toward the center of the water.

Why? In the overfilled glass, the surface water **molecules** above the glass pull on each other. The direction of this pull creates a bulge on the water's surface and pulls the paper circles toward the peak of the bulge.

91. Tug-of-War

Purpose To determine why some materials get wetter than others.

Materials   drinking glass   eyedropper
                liquid cooking oil   tap water

Procedure
1. Turn the glass upside down on a table and rub a drop of oil on one half of its bottom surface.
2. Fill the eyedropper with water and squeeze a drop of water on both the oiled and the unoiled areas of the glass.
3. Observe the shape of the water drops.

Results The water drop spreads out and flattens on the clean surface of the glass. The drop of water on the oiled surface is more ball-like in shape.

Why? The shape of the water drops is due to two different forces, cohesion and adhesion. **Cohesion** is the force of attraction between like **molecules**, such as water molecules. The water molecules pull on each other, which gives the drops of liquid a **spherical** (ball-like) shape. **Adhesion** is the force of attraction between different kinds of molecules, such as glass and water molecules. Glass strongly attracts the water mol-

ecules, which causes the water drop to flatten and spread out. Water is said to "wet" a surface if it spreads out on the material. The wetting ability of water depends on the adhesive force between the surface molecules and the water molecules. The adhesion between an oily surface and water molecules is very small, and thus a drop of water on an oily surface retains its spherical shape.

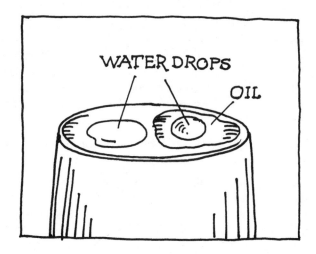

92. Uphill Climbers

Purpose To determine if water can rise in a vertical paper towel.

Materials   scissors
                2-by-8-inch (5-by-20-cm) strip of paper towel
                red food coloring
                transparent tape
                pencil
                tap water
                ruler
                glass jar, about 6 inches (15 cm) tall

Procedure
1. Place a drop of red food coloring 2 inches (5 cm) from one end of the paper strip.
2. Tape the uncolored end of the paper to the center of the pencil. Roll some of the paper around the pencil.
3. Pour about 1 inch (2.5 cm) of water into the jar.
4. Lower the paper into the jar. Unroll the strip until the bottom edge just touches the water.

Results The water dissolves the red coloring as it rises in the paper strip. The red coloring spreads outward and upward.

Why? The paper is made of tiny fibers. The spacing of the fibers forms tubelike structures throughout the paper. The water can be seen zigzagging through these spaces. The **adhesive** attraction of water to the paper is strong enough to move the water up the sides of the fiber tubes against the downward pull of **gravity**. The water **molecules** clinging to the fiber then pull the lower water molecules up the center of the tube. The movement of the water up through the tiny tubes is called **capillary action**.

93. Blow Up

Purpose To determine if a gas fills an open container.

Materials drinking straw
empty glass soda bottle
9-inch (22.5-cm) round balloon

Procedure
1. Hold the top of the balloon and push the bottom of the balloon inside the bottle.
2. Insert the straw into the bottle beside the balloon.
3. Blow into the mouth of the balloon.

Results The balloon inflates and air is felt coming out of the straw.

Why? The air surrounding the bottle, like all gases, is in constant motion. This moving gas enters, spreads out, and fills the open bottle and straw. As you inflate the balloon inside the bottle, it pushes against the air inside the bottle. The pressure from the balloon forces the air in the bottle out the straw.

94. Clingers

Purpose To determine if water can flow at an angle.

Materials 18-inch (45-cm) piece of cotton kite string
measuring cup with spout and handle
tap water
drinking glass
cookie sheet
helper

Procedure
1. Tie one end of the string around the top of the measuring cup's handle.
2. Fill the cup with water.
3. Wet the entire length of the string with water.
4. Set the glass in the center of the cookie sheet.
5. Lay the string over the spout of the measuring cup.
6. Ask your helper to hold the free end of the string against the inside of the glass.
7. Separate the cup and glass so the string is tight.
8. Raise the bottom of the cup about 12 inches (30 cm) above the cookie sheet.
9. Slowly pour the water out of the cup.

Results The water flows down the string into the glass.

Why? The water in the wet string attracts the **molecules** in the falling water. The **surface tension** on the outside of the flowing water holds the water close to the string as it flows down the slanted string.

95. Magic Paper

Purpose To observe the attraction between molecules.

Materials sheet of typing paper
2-by-6-inch (5-by-15-cm) piece of news-
    paper
rubber cement
talcum powder
scissors (*Do not* use school scissors.)

Procedure
1. Lay the typing paper on a table and place the newspaper in its center.
2. Evenly spread a thin, solid covering of rubber cement over the top surface of the newspaper.
3. Allow the rubber cement to dry for 5 minutes.
4. Sprinkle talcum powder evenly over the cement.
5. Cut the newspaper into two 1-by-6-inch (2.5-by-15-
cm) strips.
6. Place the strips together with the powdered surfaces touching.
7. Cut across one end of the strips by inserting the paper as far into the scissors as possible and cutting
with the largest part of the blade.
8. Gently raise the other end of one of the strips.
9. Hold up only the raised edge, allowing the strip to
hang.

Results One long strip is formed.

Why? The powder is used to cover the cement so that
the pieces do not stick together. When the sharp edges
of the scissors cut the paper, the pressure applied by
the blades pushes a small amount of rubber cement
along the cut surface. The **adhesion** between the cement **molecules** is great. These molecules are able to
bridge the gap between the cut pieces and hold them
together.

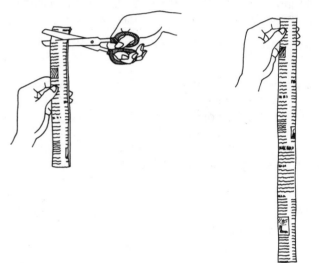

96. Escaping Bubbles

Purpose To determine why bubbles escape from a
glass of soda.

Materials baby food jar
soda, any flavor

Procedure
1. Fill the jar one-half full with soda.
2. Set the jar on a table and observe the liquid.

Results Small bubbles of gas continuously rise to the
top of the liquid.

Why? Carbonated beverages are made by dissolving
large amounts of carbon dioxide gas in flavored water.
This excess amount of carbon dioxide gas is able to
stay in the liquid because it is pushed with high pressure into the bottle and the bottle is immediately
sealed. In the open glass the pressure on the soda is
much less than in the closed bottle. Thus, carbon dioxide bubbles form in the soda, rise to the surface, and
escape into the air.

97. Expando

Purpose To observe that a gas dissolved in liquid takes up less space than undissolved gas.

Materials glass bottle of soda with a screw cap
9-inch (23-cm) balloon

Procedure

1. Remove the cap from the bottle.
2. Pour about half of the soda out of the bottle.
3. Stretch the mouth of the balloon over the mouth of the bottle.
4. Hold the balloon securely around the bottle's mouth and shake the bottle vigorously.

    NOTE: Do this outside in case the balloon comes loose and the soda spills.

5. Continue to hold the balloon securely around the bottle's mouth and hold the bottle upright.
6. Observe the balloon.

Results Foam fills the bottle and the balloon inflates.

Why? Before shaking, carbon dioxide gas was dissolved in the soda. The soda and its dissolved gas filled about half of the bottle. Shaking the soda releases the dissolved gas. As the gas quickly spreads out, it carries some of the soda with it, forming foam in the bottle. The expanding gas and some foam move into the balloon and inflate it.

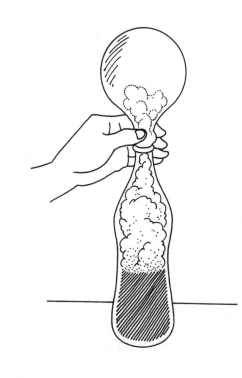

98. Limewater

Purpose To make a testing solution for carbon dioxide.

Materials 2 quart (liter) glass jars with lids
distilled water
1 tablespoon (15 ml) lime (also called
calcium oxide; used to make pickles)
spoon
masking tape
marking pen
adult helper

Procedure

1. Fill one jar with distilled water.
2. Ask an adult to add the lime to the water and stir.

    CAUTION: Do not get powdered lime in your nose or eyes. It can damage these soft tissues.

3. Place the lid securely on the jar. Allow the solution to stand overnight.
4. On the following day, pour the clear liquid into the second jar. Be careful not to pour out any of the lime that has settled on the bottom of the jar.
5. Use the tape and marking pen to label the second jar Limewater. Place the lid securely on the second jar and save it for other experiments.

Results The liquid is milky white at first. After standing overnight, the liquid is clear.

Why? The lime is a **solute** (dissolving material) and the water a **solvent** (dissolving medium). The mixing of a solute and solvent produces a **solution**. In the lime solution, the undissolved particles of lime are temporarily suspended in the water, making it appear milky. It takes time for all of the tiny particles to settle. The clear liquid is a **saturated solution**, meaning that no more solute (lime) can dissolve in the solvent (water). It must be covered to prevent the carbon dioxide in the air from dissolving in it.

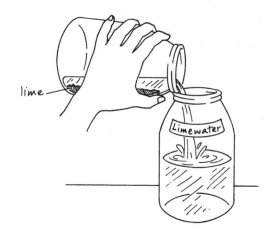

99. Producer

Purpose To observe the production of carbon dioxide by yeast.

Materials ½ package powdered yeast
2 glass soda bottles
warm tap water
1 teaspoon (5 ml) sugar
18-inch (45-cm) piece of aquarium tubing
modeling clay
limewater (from Experiment 98)

Procedure
1. Pour the yeast into one bottle and fill it half full with warm tap water.
2. Add the sugar to the bottle. Place your thumb over the bottle's mouth, and shake the bottle vigorously to mix the contents.
3. Place one end of the tubing in the top part of the bottle.
4. Use the clay to seal off the bottle and to hold the tubing in the bottle.
5. Fill the second soda bottle half full with limewater.
6. Insert the free end of the tubing into the limewater in the second bottle. Use the clay to seal off the bottle and to hold the tubing in the bottle.
7. Observe the limewater periodically for several days.

Results Bubbles of gas flow out of the tubing into the limewater. The limewater turns cloudy.

Why? Yeast is a type of **fungus** that uses sugar and oxygen to produce energy. In this chemical process of producing energy, carbon dioxide is also formed. Limewater turns cloudy when carbon dioxide gas is bubbled through it. The cloudiness of the limewater is proof that the bubbles produced by the reaction are carbon dioxide.

yeast/sugar   Limewater

100. Chemical Breath

Purpose To test for the presence of carbon dioxide gas in exhaled breath.

Materials clear drinking glass
limewater (from Experiment 98)
drinking straw

Procedure
1. Fill the glass one-fourth full with limewater.
2. Use the straw to blow into the limewater.

   CAUTION: Do not drink the limewater.

3. Continue to blow into the liquid until a distinctive color is observed.

Results The limewater turns from clear to a milky color.

Why? Limewater always turns milky when mixed with carbon dioxide. The chemical in the limewater combines with the carbon dioxide gas in the breath to form **limestone**, a white powder that does not dissolve in water. If the **solution** is allowed to stand for several hours, the powdery limestone will fall to the bottom of the glass.

101. Super Chain

Purpose To observe a physical change.

Materials lined notebook paper   scissors
pencil   ruler

Procedure

1. On the paper, draw and cut out a rectangle that is 4 inches (10 cm) wide and 12 lines long.
2. Fold the rectangle in half lengthwise, perpendicular to the lines.
3. Cut across the fold at points A and B as shown. Stop about ¼ inch (½ cm) from the edge of the paper.
4. Cut along each of the printed lines alternating from the folded edge to the open edge. Be sure to stop ¼ inch (½ cm) from the edge.
5. Start at point B and cut the folded edge off of the paper ending at point A. Do not cut the folded edge from the two ends.
6. Carefully stretch the paper open.

Results The shape of the paper changed from a rectangle to an open chain-like structure.

Why? Cutting the paper results in a **physical change** (a change that does not produce a new substance). The zigzag structure allows the paper to stretch out into a large super chain.

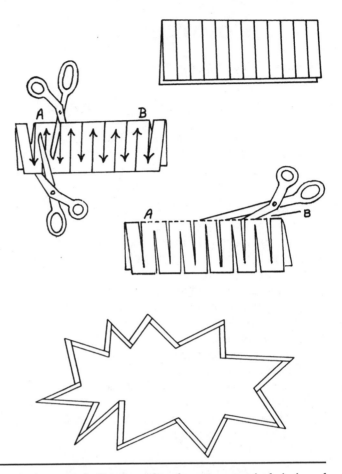

102. Breakdown

Purpose To change the natural form of an egg white.

Materials raw egg
2-quart (2-liter) bowl
fork
adult helper

Procedure

1. Ask an adult to help you separate the yolk from the egg white, placing the egg white in the bowl.
2. Allow the egg white to sit undisturbed at room temperature for 20 minutes.
3. Dip the fork into the egg white, and lift the fork above the bowl. Observe the texture and color of the egg white on the fork.
4. Return the egg white to the bowl, and with a quick whipping motion, use the fork to beat the egg white.
5. After 50 strokes, observe the egg white again.

Results Before beating, the egg white actually has a pale yellow color and a slimy texture. After beating, the color is white, and the texture is soft and foamy. The foamy egg white takes up more space than the slimy egg white.

Why? **Denaturing** means to change something from its natural form. In its natural form, the egg white contains about 85 percent water and about 10 percent protein. It is the **protein** (large **molecules** composed of chains of smaller molecules) that is denatured by the whipping action. The protein molecules are similar to balls of yarn, and beating the egg white causes the balls of proteins to unravel. The shape of this new unwound protein molecule traps air and thus forms a foam that can be three times the original size of the molecule. The color is also changed as the molecules are rearranged.

103. Colored Eggs

Purpose To determine the role of vinegar in dyeing eggshells.

Materials 1-pint (500-ml) jar   masking tape
tap water   white vinegar (5%)
measuring spoons   large spoon
blue food coloring   2 hard-boiled eggs
2 drinking glasses   paper towel
marking pen

Procedure

1. Fill the jar half full with water.
2. Add 2 teaspoons (10 ml) of food coloring to the water and stir. Pour half of the colored water into one glass and half into the other.
3. Use the tape and marking pen to label one of the glasses With Vinegar. Add 1 teaspoon (5 ml) of vinegar to this glass and stir.
4. Label the other glass Without Vinegar.
5. Use the large spoon to place one egg in each of the glasses.
6. Allow the eggs to remain undisturbed for 2 minutes.
7. Remove the eggs, place them on the paper towel, and allow them to air dry. Observe their color.

Results The egg soaked in the dye solution containing vinegar is a darker blue than the egg soaked in the dye solution without vinegar.

Why? To dye an object, the **molecules** of dye must stick to the surface of the object. Vinegar (acetic acid and water) reacts with the layer of **protein** molecules covering the surface of the eggshell so that the surface becomes positively charged and attracts the negatively charged dye molecules, causing the darker blue color. The egg in the solution without vinegar has some color because some of the dye molecules become lodged in crevices in the eggshell.

104. Wash Out!

Purpose To determine how stains are cleaned by enzymes found in detergents.

Materials 1 quart (liter) glass jar
tap water
measuring spoon
powdered laundry detergent with enzymes
large spoon
marking pen
masking tape
1 fresh, peeled hard-boiled egg
magnifying lens

Procedure

1. Fill the jar three-fourths full with tap water.
2. Add 1 tablespoon (15 ml) of the laundry detergent to the jar of water and stir.
3. Place the egg in the jar and put it in a warm area, such as near a window with direct sunlight.
4. Each day, for 7 or more days, lift the egg out of the jar with the spoon and use the magnifying lens for close-up inspection.
5. Each day, replace the eggs in a fresh solution of the mixture of laundry detergent and water.

Results The egg has large craters on its surface.

Why? Tangled strings of some **proteins** get wrapped around the fibers in clothes, causing stains. For these stains to be removed, the proteins must be broken into smaller pieces. **Enzymes**, like those in the detergent used in this experiment, are biological **catalysts** (chemicals that change the rate of a chemical reaction without being changed themselves). They cut the long strands of proteins (as they did on the surface of the egg) without affecting the cloth fibers. These cut pieces slip out of the cloth and are washed away with the dirt.

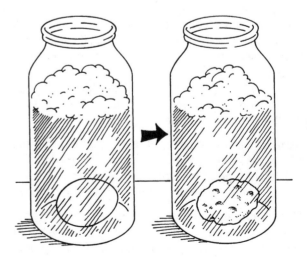

105. Rubbery

Purpose To demonstrate the effect of vinegar on bones.

Materials cooked chicken leg
quart (liter) jar with lid
white vinegar (5%)
adult helper

Procedure

1. Ask an adult to cut as much of the meat away from the chicken leg bone as possible.
2. Examine the flexibility of the bone by trying to bend it with your fingers.
3. Place the cleaned bone in the jar.
4. Cover the bone with vinegar.
5. Secure the lid on the jar.
6. After 24 hours, remove the bone from the jar and examine it for flexibility.
7. Replace the bone in the vinegar.
8. Examine the bone for flexibility each day for 7 days.

Results The flexibility of the bone increases daily. At the end of the test period, the bone feels very rubbery.

Why? Vinegar, which is an **acid**, reacts chemically with the bone. It removes the calcium compounds in the bone.

The bone becomes rubbery as the result of the loss of calcium. This indicates that calcium is the chemical element in bones that gives them strength and firmness.

106. Sweeter

Purpose To compare the sweetness of sugar and artificial sweeteners.

Materials blindfold (a long scarf will work)
packet of NutraSweet®
packet of Sweet'n Low®
packet of table sugar
plate
3 clean cotton swabs
cup of tap water
helper

Procedure

NOTE: Never taste anything in a laboratory setting unless you are sure that it does not contain harmful chemicals or materials.

1. Place the blindfold over your helper's eyes.
2. Open each packet of sweetener and pour the contents in separate piles on the plate. Lay each packet next to its sweetener to identify it.
3. Moisten a cotton swab with water, lay it on a sweetener in the plate, then hand it to your helper.
4. Instruct your helper to put the swab in his or her mouth, taste the sweetener, and note its sweetness.
5. Have your helper drink a small amount of water to rinse the sweetener out of his or her mouth.
6. Repeat steps 3 through 5 with each of the other two sweeteners. Ask your helper to compare the sweetness of each sample.

Results The sweetest-tasting sweetener is Sweet'n Low. Table sugar is the least sweet.

Why? Sweet'n Low is **saccharin**, a chemical that tastes about 300 times sweeter than **sucrose** (table sugar). The chemical **aspartame**, with the trade name NutraSweet, is about 200 times sweeter than sucrose.

107. Lumpy

Purpose To demonstrate why milk curdles.

Materials ¼ cup (63 ml) whole milk
small bowl
2 tablespoons (30 ml) white vinegar
spoon
timer

Procedure
1. Pour the milk into the bowl.
2. Add the vinegar and stir.
3. Allow the contents of the bowl to stand for about 5 minutes.

Results The milk separates into white solid lumps mixed with a thin, watery liquid. Most of the lumps sink to the bottom of the bowl.

Why? Milk contains particles of **casein** (milk **protein**). The casein particles are negatively charged. Vinegar is an **acid**; like all acids, it contains positively charged hydrogen particles. Negative and positive charges are attracted to each other. Thus, the negatively charged casein particles and the positively charged hydrogen particles combine, forming white lumps. Allowing milk to become warm produces the same results that add-ing vinegar does. The sugar in the milk changes into an acid. The positive hydrogens in the acid attract the negative casein. In both cases, the milk separates into white lumps called **curds** (the solid part of milk) and a thin watery liquid called **whey** (the liquid part of milk).

108. Faded

Purpose To determine how sunlight affects color.

Materials scissors
ruler
sheet of red construction paper
stiff paper, such as a file folder

Procedure
1. Cut a 6-by-6-inch (15-by-15-cm) square from both the construction paper and the stiff paper.
2. Cut a large star from the center of the square of stiff paper.
3. Lay the square of stiff paper, with the star section removed, over the square of red paper.
4. Place the pieces of paper near a window that receives direct sunlight.
5. After 2 days, remove the stiff paper.

Results A light red or pink star shape is in the center of the red paper.

Why? The energy from the sunlight causes some color pigments to **fade** (get lighter in color). Different chemical reactions occur when sunlight is absorbed by a substance. The fading of colors is generally the result of the combination of oxygen in the air with the color pigment. This fading happens very slowly without the sunlight, but with the sunlight, it occurs quickly.

109. Antifreezing

Purpose To show that salt makes it harder for water to freeze.

Materials 2 5-ounce (150-ml) paper cups
tap water
1 tablespoon (15 ml) table salt
marking pen
timer

Procedure
1. Fill each cup half full with water.
2. Dissolve the salt in one of the cups.
3. Label the cup containing the salt S.
4. Set both cups in the freezer.
5. Check the cups every hour for 4 hours, then again after 24 hours.

Results The water without salt freezes during the first 4 hours, but the salty water never freezes.

Why? The salt causes the water to freeze at a lower temperature. Water generally freezes at 32 degrees Fahrenheit (0°C). At this temperature, the water **molecules** cling together to form ice crystals. The presence of salt interferes with the forming of the crystals. The effect of salt's interference is overcome by lowering the temperature.

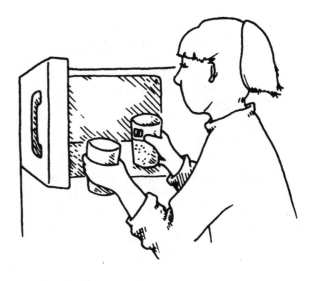

110. Cubes

Purpose To grow cubes of salt crystals.

Materials baby food jar
tap water
1½ tablespoons (22.5 ml) table salt
spoon
scissors
sheet of dark construction paper
saucer

Procedure
1. Fill the jar half full with water.
2. Add the salt to the water. Stir.
3. Cut a circle from the paper to fit the inside of the saucer.
4. Pour a thin layer of the salt solution over the paper. Try not to pour any undissolved salt onto the paper.
5. Place the saucer in a warm place.
6. Observe the paper daily for 7 or more days.

Results Small, white, cubic crystals form on the paper and increase in size every day.

Why? As the water **evaporates**, dry salt is deposited on the paper. Table salt crystals have a cubic shape.

The tiny unseen crystals are deposited first, and, as more water evaporates, the crystals stack until they are large enough to be seen.

111. Bouncy Blubber

Purpose To produce an elastic material.

Materials 1 teaspoon (5 ml) borax (a water softener found with laundry detergents in grocery stores)
1 cup (250 ml) distilled water
spoon
timer
4-ounce (120-ml) bottle of white school glue
tap water
paper towel

Procedure

1. Add the borax to the water. Stir and allow the solution to stand for 5 minutes.
2. Hold the glue bottle upside down above the cup of borax solution.
3. Squeeze the bottle so that a thin stream of glue falls into the cup. Stir continuously.
4. Stop the stream of glue when the spoon becomes covered.
5. With your hands, pull the white mass (bouncy blubber) off the spoon. Wash the mass in cold tap water.
6. Dry your hands with the paper towel. Then, gently press and roll the bouncy blubber in your hands to dry and shape it into a round ball.
7. Drop the ball on a table or hard floor.

Results The ball bounces.

Why? The bouncy blubber is **elastic**, meaning it is capable of springing back into shape after being stretched or squeezed. When the ball touches the surface of the table or floor, it flattens slightly. The more quickly it returns to its original shape, the higher it bounces.

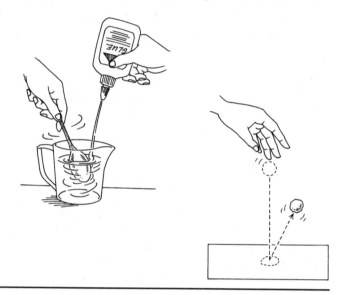

112. Dilution

Purpose To observe a color change as a solution becomes more dilute.

Materials measuring cup
tap water
1-gallon (4-liter) glass jar
red food coloring
spoon

Procedure

1. Pour ½ cup (125 ml) of water into the jar.
2. Add and stir in 1 drop of food coloring.
3. Add 1 cup (250 ml) of water at a time to the jar until the red color disappears.

Results It takes about 7 cups (1.75 liters) of clear water to make the red color disappear.

Why? The red is visible at first because the **molecules** of red color are close enough together to be seen. As clear water is added, the color molecules continue to spread evenly throughout the water. They finally get far enough apart to become invisible because of their small size. The red water has been **diluted** (thinned out or weakened by adding a solvent such as water).

113. Suspended

Purpose To observe the Tyndall effect.

Materials small cardboard box, large enough to
cover a quart (liter) jar
scissors
2 quart (liter) jars
tap water
1 teaspoon (5 ml) flour
spoon
flashlight
adult helper

Procedure

1. Ask an adult to do the following to prepare the box:
   a. Use the point of the scissors to make a small hole in the end of the box. The height of the hole should be half the height of the jars being used.
   b. Cut a 1-inch (2.5-cm) square viewing hole in front of the box. The hole must be near the corner of the box and as high as the small round hole on the side.
2. Fill the jars three-fourths full with water.
3. Add flour to one of the jars and stir.
4. Place each jar, in turn, in front of the viewing hole.
5. Ask your helper to hold the flashlight near the small hole. Observe the contents of each jar through the viewing hole.

Results The glass of flour and water looks brighter than the glass of water alone.

Why? Flour and water form a **suspension** (a mixture of a solid and a liquid in which the solid material doesn't dissolve in the liquid but temporarily stays suspended until gravity pulls it down). Light hits the bits of flour floating in the water and is **reflected**, or bounced back. The water alone does not reflect the light. Reflection of light by suspended particles is called the **Tyndall effect**, named after the British scientist, John Tyndall.

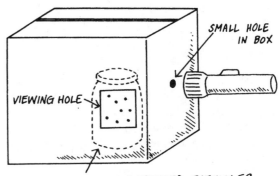

JAR WITH SUSPENDED PARTICLES

114. Separator

Purpose To separate a suspension by spinning.

Materials 24-inch (60-cm) piece of strong cord
small bucket
tap water
spoon
¼ cup (63 ml) flour
clear drinking glass

Procedure

1. Tie the ends of the cord to the handle of the bucket.
2. Fill the bucket one-fourth full with water.
3. Stir the flour into the water.
4. Carry the pail and glass outside. In an area clear of objects and people, hold the cord and swing the bucket around 15 times.
5. Pour a small amount of the liquid from the bucket into the empty glass.
6. If the liquid looks cloudy, swing the bucket 15 times again and pour another small amount of liquid into the glass.
7. Continue to swing and pour until the liquid looks clear.

Results The number of swings varies with how fast the bucket is spun, but with enough swings, the solution clears.

Why? Flour and water form a **suspension**. If standing, **gravity** would eventually cause the flour particles to separate from the water. Spinning speeds the separation process by producing a strong **centrifugal force** (an outward force exerted by an object moving in a curved path). This force pushes the floating flour particles to the bottom of the bucket.

115. Floating Spheres

Purpose To observe liquids that will and will not mix together.

Materials ½ cup (125 ml) water
clear drinking glass
liquid cooking oil
blue food coloring
pencil

Procedure
1. Pour the water into the glass.
2. Slowly add the oil until the glass is about three-fourths full.
3. Add five drops of food coloring to the glass.
4. While looking at the underside of the oil's surface, use a pencil to push the drops of coloring into the water.

Results Two separate layers form. The oil floats on top of the water. The balls of food coloring float just beneath the surface of the oil. Some of the colored balls sink and sit just above the surface of the water. When the colored balls touch the water, they break apart and dissolve in the water.

Why? Oil and water are **immiscible liquids**, meaning they do not mix and will separate into layers. Food coloring does not dissolve in oil and will float if the drops are small enough. The oil surrounding the balls of color prevents them from touching the water. Pushing the balls through the oil allows them to touch and mix with the water. Food coloring and water are **miscible liquids** (capable of being mixed).

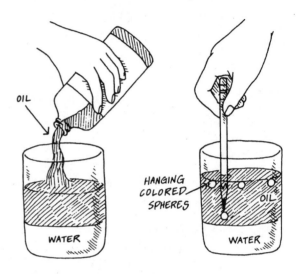

116. Stretchy

Purpose To determine how heat affects the movement of molecules in a rubber band.

Materials pencil
one 5-ounce (150-ml) paper cup
scissors
ruler
string
rubber band, about 3 inches (7.5 cm) long
salt
masking tape
hair dryer (*Use only with adult supervision.*)
adult helper

Procedure
1. Use the pencil to punch two holes under the rim of the paper cup on opposite sides.
2. Cut an 8-inch (20-cm) piece of string. Tie the ends through each hole in the cup to form a loop.
3. Cut the rubber band once to make one 6-inch (15-cm) -long strip and tie one end of the rubber band to the string loop on the cup.
4. Cut an 18-inch (45-cm) length of string and attach it to the free end of the rubber band.
5. Fill the cup about half full with salt.
6. Set the cup on the floor under the edge of a table and tape the string to the top of the table so the cup is just resting on the floor.
7. Ask an adult to hold the hair dryer turned to high heat about 2 inches (5 cm) from the rubber band and move it up and down the band.
8. Observe the position of the cup as the rubber band is heated for about 10 seconds.

Results The cup rises slightly when the rubber band is heated.

Why? Heating the rubber band causes the rubber **molecules** to **vibrate**. The moving molecules separate slightly and slip past each other, causing the band to thicken and become shorter.

117. In Motion

Purpose To determine how temperature affects dissolving substances in water.

Materials 2 ice cubes
2 small clear drinking glasses
cold and warm tap water
flat toothpick
box of flavored gelatin (flavors such as grape, cherry, or strawberry work best)

Procedure
1. Place the ice cubes in one glass and fill it with cold water.
2. Fill the other glass with warm water.
3. Use the large end of the toothpick to scoop up the flavored gelatin.
4. Observe from the side of the glass as you gently shake the gelatin over the glass of warm water.
5. Remove the ice from the first glass. Repeat steps 3 and 4 with the glass of cold water.

Results The gelatin dissolves quickly in the warm water, but most of it sinks to the bottom in the cold water.

Why? Heat causes the **molecules** of water to move faster. Thus, in the warm water, the water molecules bump into the particles of gelatin. This bumping motion quickly mixes the warm water and gelatin. The gelatin in the cold water will eventually mix because even in cold water the molecules are in motion; they just move much more slowly.

118. Hotter

Purpose To demonstrate an exothermic reaction.

Materials 5-ounce (150-ml) paper cup
small plastic spoon
plaster of paris
tap water

Procedure
1. In the paper cup, mix together 4 spoonfuls of plaster of paris with 2 spoonfuls of water.

   NOTE: Do not wash any plaster down the sink, as it can clog the drain.

2. Determine if a temperature change occurs by touching the surface of the plaster with your fingers periodically for 1 hour.

Results A very thick, cool liquid forms at first. As the liquid hardens, its temperature increases.

Why? The plaster of paris gives off energy in the form of heat as it hardens. A chemical reaction that gives off energy is called an **exothermic reaction**. Plaster of paris is made by grinding glassy-looking gypsum crystals into a powder. The powder is then heated to remove its moisture. This dry powder changes back into a crystal structure when water is added. Heat is given off during the reforming of the crystal. (Note that the chalky-looking crystal structure does not look like the original glassy structure.)

119. Colder

Purpose To demonstrate an endothermic reaction.

Materials thermometer
$\frac{1}{4}$ cup (63 ml) cold tap water
timer
2 effervescent antacid tablets

Procedure
1. Stand the thermometer in the cup of water.
2. After 5 minutes, note the temperature of the water.
3. Place the antacid tablets in the water near the bulb of the thermometer.
4. When the tablets stop fizzing, observe the temperature of the water and note any change.

Results The temperature of the water lowers.

Why? The reaction of the antacid tablets with water requires energy. A reaction that absorbs energy is called an **endothermic reaction**. The energy for this reaction is absorbed from the water; consequently, the water gets colder.

120. Cabbage Indicator

Purpose To prepare a cabbage indicator that can be used to test for acids and bases.

Materials red cabbage quart (liter) jar with lid
food blender masking tape
distilled water marking pen
tea strainer adult helper
large bowl

Procedure
1. Fill the blender half way with cabbage leaves, then cover them with distilled water.
2. Ask an adult to blend the water and cabbage.
3. Ask your helper to strain the contents of the blender into the bowl.
4. Pour the cabbage juice from the bowl into the jar. Label the jar Cabbage Indicator.
5. Close the lid on the jar and store it in the refrigerator until needed for Experiments 121, 122, and 123.

Results The juice from the cabbage is purple.

Why? The blender breaks open the cells of the cabbage, and the colored chemicals inside the cells mix with the water. The juice that forms can be used to indicate the presence of an **acid** (substance that turns cabbage indicator a pink-to-red color) or a **base** (substance that turns cabbage indicator a blue-to-green color).

121. Acid Testing

Purpose To use cabbage indicator to identify an acid.

Materials 2 tablespoons (30 ml) cabbage indicator
(from Experiment 120)
white saucer
1 teaspoon (5 ml) pickle juice
spoon

Procedure
1. Place the cabbage indicator in the saucer.
2. Observe the color of the cabbage indicator.
3. Add the pickle juice to the indicator. Stir.
4. Observe the color of the liquid in the saucer.

Results The cabbage indicator changes from purple to red when mixed with pickle juice.

Why? Cabbage indicator always turns a pink-to-red color when mixed with an **acid**. Pickle juice contains vinegar, which is an acid. The chemical name for vinegar is acetic acid.

122. Base Testing

Purpose To use cabbage indicator to identify a base.

Materials 2 tablespoons (30 ml) cabbage indicator
(from Experiment 120)
white saucer
antacid tablet
spoon
timer

Procedure
1. Place the cabbage indicator in the saucer.
2. Observe the color of the cabbage indicator.
3. Add the antacid tablet to the indicator and allow it to sit for 2 to 3 minutes. Stir.
4. Observe the color of the liquid in the saucer.

Results The cabbage indicator changes from purple to blue or green when mixed with the antacid tablet.

Why? Cabbage indicator turns a blue-to-green color when mixed with a **base**. Thus, the antacid tablet is a base. The colors blue and green indicate the amount of base. Green indicates a greater amount.

123. A or B?

Purpose To identify the presence of an acid or a base in different materials.

Materials measuring spoon
      cabbage indicator (from Experiment 120)
      white saucer
      testing materials [1 teaspoon (5 ml) of each]:
          grapefruit juice
          orange juice
          lemon juice
          baking soda
      tap water
      paper towels

Procedure

1. Place 2 tablespoons (15 ml) of the cabbage indicator in the saucer.
2. Add the grapefruit juice to the cabbage indicator.
3. Observe any color change in the cabbage indicator.
4. Repeat steps 1 through 3 for each of the three remaining testing materials, rinsing and drying the saucer thoroughly before each test.

Results All of the materials produce a pink-to-red color, except baking soda, which produces a green color.

Why? Cabbage indicator always changes to the same colors in the presence of an **acid** or a **base**. The green color produced by baking soda indicates that it is a base. The red tones produced by the other materials indicate that they are acids.

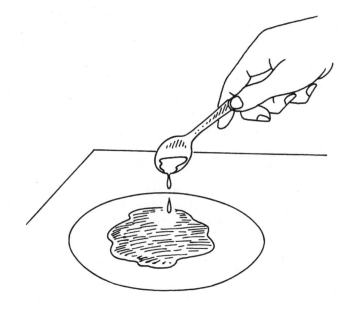

124. Baking with Acid?

Purpose To determine the importance of acid in making cake or bread rise.

Materials pencil   4 paper cups
         2 sheets of paper   baking soda
         measuring spoon   tap water
         baking powder   white vinegar

Procedure

1. Write Baking Powder on one sheet of paper and Baking Soda on the other. Lay the papers on a table.
2. Put 1 teaspoon (5 ml) of baking powder in each of two of the cups. Place them on the paper labeled Baking Powder.
3. Clean the spoon and put 1 teaspoon (5 ml) of baking soda in each of the remaining two cups. Place them on the paper labeled Baking Soda.
4. Add 2 tablespoons (30 ml) of water to cups 1 and 3. Note the contents of the cups.
5. Add 2 tablespoons (30 ml) of vinegar to cups 2 and 4. Note the contents of the cups.

Results Foam is produced in cups 1, 2, and 4. Cup 3 produces a thick milky-looking solution.

Why? The foam that is produced in cups 1, 2, and 4 is carbon dioxide gas mixed with liquid. Baking soda will produce carbon dioxide gas if mixed with an **acid**, such as vinegar. Baking powder is a mixture of baking soda, acid, and other materials. Water activates the powdered acid, which mixes with the baking soda to produce carbon dioxide. Carbon dioxide is needed to make a cake or bread rise during baking. The carbon dioxide pushes the batter up, and then the heat of the oven dries the batter in this elevated position.

IV
Earth Science

125. Megaweight

Purpose To demonstrate the difference in the weights of the atmosphere, hydrosphere, and lithosphere.

Materials   large paper clip
4-by-12-inch (10-by-30-cm) piece of cardboard
2 rubber bands
pencil
7-ounce (210-ml) paper cup
12-inch (30-cm) piece of string
marking pen
tap water
soil

Procedure

1. Attach the paper clip to the center of one of the short sides of the cardboard. Tie the rubber bands together and hang them on the paper clip.
2. Use the pencil to punch two holes on opposite sides of the cup just under the rim.
3. Loop the string through the rubber band and tie the ends through each hole in the cup.
4. Hold the cardboard so that the cup hangs freely.
5. Let the bottom of the lower rubber band be the pointer. Mark the position of the pointer and label the mark Air.

6. Fill the cup with water. Mark the position of the pointer and label the mark Water.
7. Empty the cup and refill it with soil. Mark the position of the pointer and label the mark Land.

Results Comparing the weight of equal quantities of air, water, and soil indicates that air is the lightest and soil is the heaviest of the three materials.

Why? The **lithosphere** is the outer part of the earth, not including the air above the earth (the **atmosphere**) or the water on the earth (the **hydrosphere**). This experiment indicates that soil is heavier than air or water.

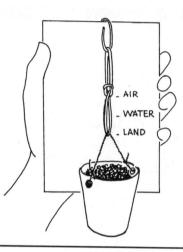

126. Rainbow

Purpose To determine how the sun's position affects how a rainbow is made.

Materials garden hose with sprayer

Procedure

NOTE: Since there is a possibility of getting wet, the best time to perform this experiment is on a warm day.

CAUTION: Never look directly at the sun.

1. Turn the water on and adjust the nozzle on the hose so that it sprays a fine mist of water.
2. Stand with the sun behind you and look for a rainbow in the water spray.
3. Turn around so that the sun is in front of you, and look for a rainbow in the water spray, again.

Results A rainbow can be seen only when the sun is behind you.

Why? A rainbow is an arc of colors in the sky. To see a rainbow, there must be water droplets in the air in front of you and the sun must be shining behind you. When sunlight passes through a raindrop, it is **refracted** or bent, and the light separates into seven colors: red, orange, yellow, green, blue, indigo, and violet. All rainbows are part of a circle, but only part of the circle is visible, because the earth is in the way.

127. Dripper

Purpose To demonstrate the formation of stalagmites and stalactites.

Materials 2 baby food jars
Epsom salt
tap water
spoon
2 washers
18-inch (45-cm) piece of cotton string
sheet of dark construction paper

Procedure

NOTE: This activity works best in humid weather.

1. Fill each jar with Epsom salt. Add just enough water to cover the Epsom salt and stir.
2. Tie a washer to each end of the string.
3. Place one washer in each of the jars and place the sheet of paper between the jars.
4. Position the jars so that the string hangs between them with the lowest part of the loop about 1 inch (2.5 cm) above the paper.
5. Allow the jars to stand undisturbed and out of any draft for 1 week or longer.

Results Water drips from the center of the loop onto the paper. A hard, white crust forms on the string and grows down as time passes. A mound of white crystals builds up on the paper beneath the string.

Why? Water containing Epsom salt moves through the string. As the water **evaporates**, crystals of Epsom salt are deposited. The Epsom salt formations are models of how crystal deposits form in caves. **Stalactites** are icicle-shaped crystals that hang from a cave's roof. **Stalagmites** are crystals that build up from the floor of the cave.

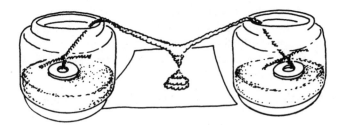

128. Gulp!

Purpose To demonstrate one way that fossils become embedded in ice.

Materials cake pan
tap water
heavy rock, about the size of your fist

Procedure
1. Fill the cake pan with water. Place the pan in the freezer overnight to allow the water to freeze.
2. When the ice is frozen, leave the pan in the freezer and place the rock on top of the ice.
3. Gently lift the rock once a day for 3 or more days.

Results At first the rock can be lifted, but then it sinks into the ice. The ice sticks to the rock, making it difficult to lift.

Why? At first the rock is hotter than the ice. The heat of the rock causes the ice to melt, and the rock sinks. After the rock cools, it continues to sink very slowly into the ice. The weight of the rock pushes down on the ice, causing it to melt. The liquid water is cold enough to refreeze around the rock. **Fossils** (traces of the remains of prehistoric animals and plants) are found deeply embedded in ice, mainly because falling snow covered the organism, but also because the weight of the animal caused it to sink through the ice as the rock did on the pan of ice. The pressure of the organism melted the ice beneath it, and the cold water refroze as the plant or animal sank deeper into the ice.

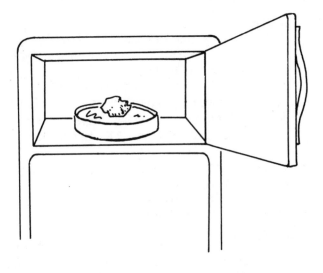

129. Fossil Dig

Purpose To demonstrate how rock can be removed from around a fossil.

Materials paper towel
chocolate-chip cookie
flat toothpick
art brush

Procedure

1. Lay the paper towel on a table.
2. Place the cookie in the center of the paper towel.
3. Follow these steps to remove a chocolate chip from the cookie without scratching the chips or breaking the cookie:
   - Use the pointed end of the toothpick to scratch away the cookie around the chocolate chip. Scratch away from the chip and never toward it.
   - With the brush, gently brush away the loose pieces of cookie.

Results The chocolate chip is removed from the cookie.

Why? **Fossils** found in relatively soft rock can often be removed in a manner similar to the way in which you removed the chocolate chip from the cookie. Instead of a

toothpick, an instrument with a metal point is used to flake away rock surrounding the fossil. The rule is always to work away from the fossil. That way, if you slip, only the unwanted rock is scratched and not the fossil. The loosened rock particles are then removed with a stiff-bristled brush.

130. Ticker

Purpose To demonstrate how sound is used to find petroleum.

Materials 2 sheets of typing paper   index card
transparent tape   helper
timer
hardcover book

Procedure

1. Roll and tape the sheets of paper to form two large tubes. Set the timer for 5 or more minutes and place it in the end of one of the tubes.
2. Tape the index card to the table as shown.
3. Position and tape the tubes to the table so that they lie along the sides of the index card with the empty tube extending about 1 inch (2.5 cm) past the edge of the table.
4. Place your ear next to the open tube and note the sound of the ticking timer.
5. While listening to the timer, ask your helper to stand the book next to the open ends of the tubes.

Results The ticking is louder with the book in place.

Why? Sound waves can be **reflected** off solids, such as the book or rock layers. Scientists are able to determine the type and hardness of rock layers beneath the

earth's surface by sending down sound waves and listening to the reflected sound. The hardness of rocks can be determined by the loudness of the reflected sound. Scientists know the hardness of rock where petroleum is found, and thus can use this method to find petroleum.

131. Shifting

Purpose To demonstrate continental separation.

Materials 2 cups (500 ml) soil
quart (liter) bowl
tap water
spoon
cookie sheet

Procedure
1. Pour the soil into the bowl.
2. Add water and stir until you have a thick mud.
3. Pour the mud onto the cookie sheet.
4. Set the pan of mud in the sun for 2 to 3 days.
5. Push down around the sides of the dried mud.

Results The surface of the dried mud cake cracks.

Why? The mud is broken into pieces with jagged edges, and all the pieces fit together. The continents of the earth, like the mud cake, look like large jigsaw-puzzle pieces. The coastlines of the continents have irregular shapes that appear to fit together. In the past, pressures within the earth may have broken a large land mass into the pieces that now form the separate continents on the earth.

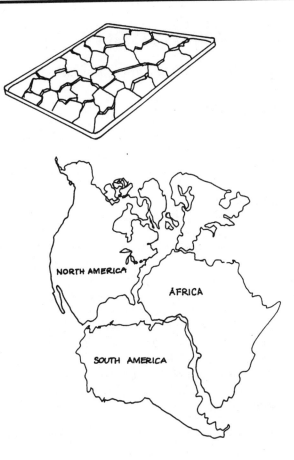

132. Pop Top

Purpose To demonstrate how a geyser works.

Materials large coffee can
tap water
funnel, as tall as the coffee can
1-yard (1-m) piece of plastic tubing

Procedure
1. Fill the can with water.
2. Set the funnel in the can, with the wide end at the bottom.
3. Place the end of the plastic tubing into the water and under the rim of the funnel.
4. Blow into the tubing.

Results Water sprays out the funnel's tube.

Why? Blowing air under the funnel forces air bubbles up the stem of the funnel. As the air moves upward, it pushes water out the top of the tube. **Geysers** are inverted funnel-shaped cracks in the earth that are filled by underground streams. When water in the lower part of the crack is heated to boiling, the bubbles of steam rise to the surface. A geyser erupts when water trapped in the neck of the funnel-shaped crack is forced out the top by the rising bubbles of steam. As long as you continue to blow under the funnel, water erupts out the top, but natural geysers erupt only when enough pressure builds up to force the water up and out the top of the crack.

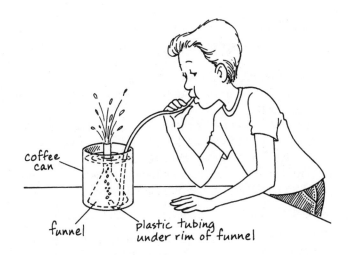

133. Widening

Purpose To demonstrate the expansion of the Atlantic Ocean.

Materials scissors
ruler
sheet of typing paper
shoe box
modeling clay

Procedure

1. Cut two 3-by-11-inch (7-by-28-cm) strips from the paper.
2. Cut out a ½-by-3½-inch (1-by-9-cm) slit from the center of the bottom of the shoe box, as shown in the diagram.
3. Cut out a 3-by-6-inch (7.5-by-15-cm) section in the center of one of the box's largest sides.
4. Put the paper strips together, and run them up through the slit in the box. Pull the strips out about 3 inches (7.5 cm), fold them back on opposite sides, and place a piece of clay on the end of each strip.
5. Hold the papers under the box and slowly push the strips up through the slit.

Results The clay pieces move away from each other.

Why? The clay represents continents bordering the Atlantic Ocean. The rising paper acts like the hot, molten rock moving out of the crack in the mid-ocean ridge. When liquid rock pushes through the ocean floor's surface, it forms a new layer on both sides of the crack. It is believed that this new material pushes against the old floor, causing it to spread apart.

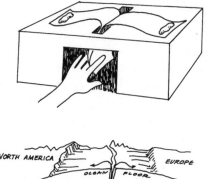

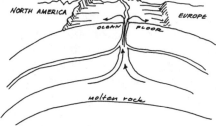

---

134. Squeezed

Purpose To determine how compression forces can bend layers of rock.

Materials 2 large thin sponges
tap water

Procedure

1. Moisten the sponges with water to make them flexible.
2. Lay the moist sponges on top of each other.
3. Place your hands on opposite ends of the sponge "sandwich."
4. While holding the "sandwich" in front of you, slowly push the ends about 2 inches (5 cm) toward the center. The sponge "sandwich" will fold up or down.
5. Repeat step 4, but tilt your hands a little to make the "sandwich" fold in the opposite direction.

Results The sponge "sandwich" folds up and down.

Why? Pushing from opposite directions causes the sponges to be squeezed into shapes representing **folds** (bends in rock layers). The result is a surface with a wavelike appearance. Forces pushing toward each other from opposite directions are called **compression forces**. Compression forces within the earth can crush rocks, or can slowly bend rock layers into folds like those of the sponge "sandwich." Folds curving upward are called **anticlines** and downward curved folds are called **synclines**.

135. Jolted

Purpose To determine how faults produce earthquakes.

Materials 2 wooden blocks, each about 2 by 4 by 6 inches (5 by 10 by 15 cm)
2 sheets of medium-grade sandpaper
masking tape

Procedure

1. Wrap each wooden block with a sheet of sandpaper, and secure with tape.
2. Hold one block in each hand. The blocks should be held straight up and down.
3. Push the blocks together tightly.
4. While continuing to push the blocks together, try to slide the blocks in different directions.

Results The sandpaper-covered blocks temporarily lock together and then move with a jolt.

Why? The **lithosphere** is broken into huge moving pieces referred to as **tectonic plates**. Where the edges of two plates push against each other, the crack between the plates is called a **fault**. **Friction** causes the plates to be temporarily locked together. Faults that are temporarily locked together are called **lock faults**. The two blocks of wood represent two tectonic plates pushing against each other. They temporarily lock together, but as with actual tectonic plates, the friction between the blocks eventually fails, causing a sudden jolt. The bond holding a locked fault in place is under tremendous stress but may last for years before suddenly slipping. Lock faults inevitably and frequently fail, resulting in an explosion of motion that produces powerful **earthquakes** (shaking of the earth caused by sudden movement of rock beneath the surface).

136. Bang!

Purpose To determine how earthquake waves (P-waves) are transmitted through the earth.

Materials scissors
ruler
string
masking tape
5 marbles

Procedure

1. Cut five 12-inch (30-cm) pieces of string.
2. Tape one string to each of the marbles.
3. Tape the free end of each string to the edge of a table. Adjust the position and length of the strings so that the marbles are at the same height and are side by side.
4. Pull one of the end marbles to the side, and then release it.
5. Observe any movement of the marbles.

Results The marble swings down, striking the closest marble in its path, and stops moving. The marble on the opposite end swings outward, and strikes its closest neighboring marble when it swings back into its original position. The cycle of the end marbles swinging back and forth continues for a few seconds.

Why? The transfer of energy from one marble to the next simulates the movement of energy from the blow of a seismic **P-wave** (primary earthquake wave) as it travels through the earth's interior. P-waves move through liquids and solids by **compressing** (pushing together) the material directly in front of them. Each compressed particle quickly springs back to its original position as soon as the energy moves on. The **crust** (outer layer of the earth's surface) moves upward as it is hit with the energy of the P-wave, and then settles back into place when the energy moves on.

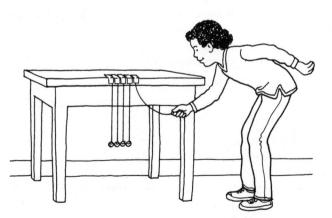

137. S-Waves

Purpose   To determine how S-waves move through the earth's interior.

Materials   6-foot (2-m) piece of rope

Procedure
1. Tie one end of the rope to a doorknob.
2. Hold the free end of the rope in your hand.
3. Back away from the door until the rope is straight.
4. Gently shake the rope up and down.
5. Gently shake the rope from side to side.

Results   Vertical and horizontal S-shaped waves form along the length of the rope.

Why?   Earthquakes produce **seismic waves** (earthquake vibrations) that move through the body of the earth toward its surface. These seismic waves inside the earth are called **body waves**. The most energetic and fastest body waves are **P-waves**, which travel at about 5 miles (8 km) per second.

S-waves (secondary waves) are slower body waves that travel at about 2 miles (3.2 km) per second beneath the earth's surface, and arrive 5 to 7 minutes after P-waves. Energy from S-waves moves away from

the source of vibrations, causing the rock layers to ripple in the same way that the ripples moved along the rope. This up-and-down or side-to-side motion is called a **transverse wave**.

138. Side-to-Side

Purpose   To determine how buildings respond to lateral (side-to-side) movements produced by earthquakes.

Materials   sheet of coarse (rough) sandpaper
Slinky

Procedure
1. Place the sandpaper on a table.
2. Stand the Slinky on end on the sandpaper.
3. Grab the edge of the sandpaper with your fingers, and quickly pull the paper about 6 inches (15 cm) toward the side of the table.
4. Observe the movement of the Slinky.

Results   The bottom of the Slinky is pulled to the side. The top section of the Slinky temporarily lags behind, and then springs back into place.

Why?   The bottom of the Slinky is pulled to the side by the movement of the paper beneath it. A similar movement occurs during an **earthquake**, when the ground below a building moves **laterally** (sideways). These lateral movements are very destructive, since they cause the walls to bend to one side. **Inertia** holds the upper part of the Slinky or a building in a leaning position for a fraction of a second, and then the structures snap back

into their original shapes. During a typical earthquake lasting only 15 seconds, a building may bend and snap between 15 and 100 times, depending on its structure.

139. Tilting

Purpose To determine how a tiltmeter gives clues to when a volcanic eruption is likely to occur.

Materials pencil
two 5-ounce (150-ml) paper cups
drinking straw
modeling clay
shallow baking pan
tap water

Procedure
1. Use the pencil to make a hole through the side of each paper cup near the bottom edge. The holes must be small enough so that the straw will fit tightly.
2. Insert about ½ inch (1.25 cm) of one end of the straw into each hole and seal with the clay.
3. Set the pan on a table and place the connected cups in the center of the pan.
4. Fill both cups half full with water.
5. Lift one end of the pan so that it is about 2 inches (5 cm) above the table. Observe the contents of each cup.

Results Raising the pan causes the amount of water to decrease in the elevated cup and to increase in the lower cup.

Why? The cups are a model of a **tiltmeter** (an instrument that measures the tilting of the ground). **Volcanologists** (scientists who study volcanoes) place the tiltmeter on a volcano, with one end pointing toward the volcano's cone and the other end pointing away. A swelling in the volcano is detected when the water content in the end pointing toward the cone decreases. An unusually large swelling in a short period of time tells scientists that an eruption is most likely on the way.

140. Riser

Purpose To determine how density affects the movement of magma.

Materials tap water
quart (liter) jar with lid
red food coloring
spoon
1 cup (250 ml) vegetable oil
timer

Procedure
1. Pour the water into the jar.
2. Add 10 drops of the food coloring and stir.
3. Slowly add the oil.
4. Secure the lid.
5. Hold the jar so that the light from a window shines through the liquid in the jar.
6. Slowly turn the jar until it is upside down, and then return it to its original position.
7. Observe and record the movement of the contents inside the jar for about 30 seconds.

Results When you first pour the oil into the jar, it floats on top of the colored water. After you tip the jar, most of the oil immediately rises again to rest above the colored water, and small bubbles of oil continue to rise for a short period of time.

Why? The separation of the two liquids is due to their being **immiscible**, meaning they do not mix. The differences in the **densities** (a comparison of the "heaviness" of materials) of the water and oil result in the denser water sinking to the bottom and the less dense oil floating to the top. Like the oil, **magma** (hot, liquid rock), which is less dense than the rock around it, tends to rise to the surface. Magma begins its upward movement from depths of 35 to 50 miles (56 to 80 km) beneath the earth's crust. This upward journey can be caused by pressures within the earth, but more often magma rises because its density is lower than that of surrounding material.

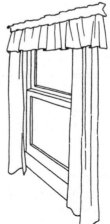

141. Spud Launcher

Purpose To determine what happens when magma hardens inside a volcano.

Materials knife (to be used only by an adult)
potato
2-liter soda bottle
½ cup (125 ml) white vinegar
dish towel
rubber band
scissors
ruler
bathroom tissue
1 teaspoon (5 ml) baking soda
adult helper

Procedure
1. Ask an adult to use the knife to prepare a potato that fits securely in the bottle.
2. Pour the vinegar into the bottle.
3. For safety, fold the towel around the bottle, leaving only the mouth of the bottle exposed. Secure with the rubber band.
4. Cut a 3-inch (7.5-cm) strip of bathroom tissue, and spread the baking soda across its center.
5. Roll the tissue around the baking soda. Secure the packet by twisting the ends of the tissue.

6. Drop the packet of baking soda into the bottle and stopper the bottle with the potato cork.
7. Stand about 1 yard (1 m) away from the bottle and observe.

Results The potato cork pops out of the bottle.

Why? The baking soda and vinegar mix together, producing carbon dioxide gas. The gas pressure pushes the cork out of the bottle. This experiment can be related to the eruption of a volcano that has a hardened plug of **magma** in the top of its vent which prevents gas from bubbling to the surface and escaping. As in the bottle, the trapped gas builds up pressure until finally the magma plug is blown out.

142. Fire Rocks

Purpose To determine what type of rock is formed when lava cools.

Materials small box with lid
marbles

Procedure
1. Cover the bottom of the box with a single layer of marbles. The marbles should fit together loosely.
2. Close the lid on the box.
3. Using both hands, lift the box and, while holding the lid secure, shake the box vigorously up and down, then side to side.
4. Quickly set the box on a table, open the lid, and observe the position of the marbles inside.

Results Shaking the box moves the marbles, leaving them in a disorderly arrangement.

Why? As the temperature of liquid rock within the earth increases, the movement of the **molecules** in the rock increases. The movement of **magma molecules** is symbolized in this experiment by the movement of the marbles as the box is shaken. During volcanic eruptions, liquid rock reaches the earth's surface and cools quickly in a matter of days or even hours. Magma that reaches the earth's surface is called **lava**. This rapid

cooling of lava means that the molecules don't have time to move into orderly patterns before the rock solidifies. This produces **igneous rock** (rock formed from molten rock). (*Igneous* is a Latin word meaning *fire*.) If the rock is formed by the solidification of lava poured out onto the earth's surface, it is called an **extrusive igneous rock**.

143. Squirt!

Purpose To demonstrate the action of a shield volcano.

Materials pencil
half-empty tube of toothpaste

Procedure
1. Use the point of a pencil to make a hole in the tube near the cap.
2. Hold the toothpaste tube in your hands.
3. With the cap screwed on tight, push against the tube to force the toothpaste toward the capped end.

Results The toothpaste slowly emerges from the hole and flows down the side of the tube.

Why? The pressure from your fingers forces the liquid toothpaste out the opening. Tremendous pressure within the earth forces **magma** out of cracks or weak spots in the earth's surface. The liquid rock is called magma when it is within the earth, but it is called **lava** once it reaches the surface. The lava cools and hardens on the surface, forming a mound of rock around the opening. A new layer is added to the mound with each eruption. This layered mound of lava is called a **shield volcano**.

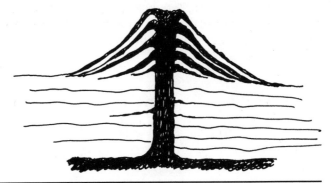

144. Wash Away

Purpose To demonstrate hydraulic mining.

Materials enough small pebbles to line the bottom of the coffee can
1 cup (250 ml) soil
coffee can
spoon
garden hose with spray nozzle

Procedure
1. Place the pebbles and soil in the can. Mix thoroughly.
2. Place the can outside on the ground.
3. Set the nozzle on the hose at the high-pressure position and direct the stream of water into the can.
4. Continue to spray the water into the can until the overflow water looks clean.

Results The soil is washed out of the can, leaving the pebbles in the bottom of the can.

Why? Some of the soil dissolves in the water and some of it is light enough to be lifted and carried out of the can by the moving water. The pebbles are too hard to be broken apart by the spraying water. The heavier materials are not lifted by the water, so they remain in the bottom of the can. Rocks that contain metal that can be mined at a profit are called **ores**. Ore deposits are mined with water. Powerful streams of water are used to wash away the soil surrounding the ore. The rock pieces left are taken to refining plants where pure metals are removed. The process of mining with water is called **hydraulic mining**.

145. Shaping

Purpose To demonstrate how land is shaped by abrasion.

Materials fingernail file
6-sided pencil

Procedure
1. Rub the file back and forth across the ridges on the pencil.
2. Observe the surface of the pencil.

Results The ridge of the pencil is cut down.

Why? The file has a rough, grainy surface. Tiny pieces are cut from the pencil as the file moves back and forth across it. Surfaces can be pitted and polished by sand grains carried by wind. The grains of sand act like the file as they strike and **erode** (wear away) surfaces. This type of erosion is called **abrasion**.

146. Weathering

Purpose To demonstrate rock weathering due to falling water.

Materials sponge
sink with a faucet
bar of soap

Procedure
1. Place the sponge in the sink under the faucet.
2. Put the bar of soap on top of the sponge.
3. For 1 day, use the faucet as usual, allowing the water to hit the center of the soap.

Results An indentation forms in the soap where the water hits it.

Why? The falling water hits the soap, knocking tiny particles free. Eventually the entire bar of soap will dissolve and wash away. Rocks at the bottom of waterfalls are slowly **weathered** (broken down into smaller pieces by natural processes). These rocks are much harder than the bar of soap and are not very soluble in water, but eventually the constant force of water hitting their surfaces breaks the rocks apart.

147. Speedy

Purpose To demonstrate how the speed of running water affects the wearing away of soil.

Materials pencil
    paper cup
    scissors
    drinking straw
    modeling clay
    cookie sheet
    ruler
    soil
    1-gallon (4-liter) plastic jug, filled with tap water

Procedure

1. Use the pencil to make a hole in the side of the paper cup near the bottom.
2. Cut the straw in half and insert one of the pieces into the hole in the cup. Seal around the hole with clay.
3. Lay the cookie sheet on the ground and raise one end about 2 inches (5 cm) by putting soil under it.
4. Cover the sheet with a thin layer of soil. Set the cup on the sheet as shown.
5. Hold your finger over the end of the straw as you fill the cup with water.
6. Release the end of the straw and observe the movement of the water.
7. Repeat steps 4 through 6, raising the end of the sheet about 6 inches (15 cm). Keep the materials for Experiment 148.

Results More soil is washed away when the slope of the cookie sheet is increased.

Why? As the slope increases, the water flows more quickly. The faster the water moves, the more energy it has, and thus the more soil it pushes forward. The process of being worn away by water is called **erosion**.

148. Wander

Purpose To determine why streams are not always straight.

Materials materials from Experiment 147
    several small rocks

Procedure

1. On the cookie sheet from Experiment 147, push one rock into the soil directly in front of the straw.
2. Continue to fill the cup with water until the running water cuts a definite path in the soil.
3. Change the direction of the stream by placing rocks in the path of the water.

Results A winding stream is cut through the soil.

Why? Obstacles that cannot be moved by the water change the direction of the stream. Water is routed around the rocks on the cookie sheet, just as it is routed around rocks in streams. Water moves in the direction of least resistance, and the soft soil is easily moved. The shape of waterways is altered by obstacles, such as rocks, and materials that cannot be moved or dissolved easily by the moving water.

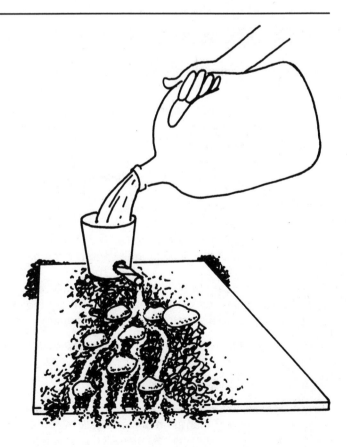

149. Fill It Up

Purpose   To demonstrate that air takes up space.

Materials   large bowl, deeper than the height of the plastic drinking glasses
tap water
masking tape
marking pen
two 7-ounce (210-ml) clear plastic drinking glasses

Procedure

1. Fill the bowl about three-fourths full with water.
2. Use the tape and marking pen to label the glasses A and B.
3. Put glass A into the water on its side, so that it fills up with water.
4. Turn the filled glass A upside down in the bowl.
5. Hold glass B upside down above the water and, keeping it straight, push it completely under the water.
6. Move glasses A and B together and slightly tilt their mouths toward each other. The edge of glass B should be under the rim of glass A, so that the bubbles from glass B rise into glass A.

Results   Glass A fills with air and glass B fills with water.

Why?   When glass B is pushed into the water, the air inside the glass prevents the water from entering the glass. Bubbles of air from glass B rise in the water because air is lighter than water. The rising air bubbles push the water out and fill glass A. Water moves into glass B to take up the space that was occupied by the air.

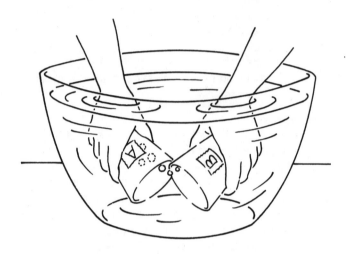

150. Downdraft

Purpose   To observe the effect of cool temperature on air movement.

Materials   drawing compass
tissue paper
scissors
transparent tape
12-inch (3-cm) piece of thread

Procedure

1. Use the compass to draw a 3-inch (7.5-cm) circle on the tissue paper.
2. Cut the circle into a spiral as shown.
3. Tape one end of the thread to the center of the paper spiral.
4. Open the refrigerator door about 8 inches (30 cm).
5. Holding the free end of the thread, hold the paper spiral just inside the bottom of the door opening.

NOTE: *Keep the spiral from this activity for Experiment 151.*

Results   The paper spiral twirls.

Why?   Cold air **molecules** have less energy and move around more slowly than do more energetic warm air molecules. The slow-moving cold air molecules tend not to move away from each other. Therefore, cold air, with its slow molecules spaced close together, is heavier than warm air, with its speedy molecules spread apart. This causes colder, heavier air to sink, and warmer, lighter air to rise. Sinking air is called a **downdraft** and rising air is called an **updraft**. The downdraft from the refrigerator hits the spiral, causing it to turn.

151. Updraft

Purpose To determine the effect of warm temperature on air movement.

Materials spiral from Experiment 150
package of instant hot chocolate
coffee cup
1 cup (250 ml) tap water
spoon
adult helper

Procedure
1. Ask an adult to prepare a cup of hot chocolate.
2. Hold the end of the thread and position the bottom of the paper spiral about 2 inches (10 cm) above the cup of hot chocolate.

Results The paper spiral twirls.

Why? The energy from the hot drink heats the air above it. The air **molecules** directly above the cup move faster and farther apart as they absorb energy. The separation of the molecules makes the air lighter and its rises upward. This upward movement of air is called an **updraft**. The updraft hits the spiral and causes it to twirl.

152. Sea Breezes

Purpose To determine the cause of sea breezes.

Materials ruler
tap water
2 glasses, large enough to hold the thermometers
soil
2 thermometers
timer
desk lamp

Procedure
1. Pour 2 inches (6 cm) of water into the first glass.
2. Pour 2 inches (6 cm) of soil into the second glass.
3. Place a thermometer in each glass.
4. Set the glasses together on a table. Allow them to stand for 30 minutes before recording the reading on each thermometer.
5. Position the lamp so that the light evenly hits both glasses.
6. After 1 hour, turn the lamp off and compare the temperatures on the thermometers.

Results The temperature of the soil is higher than the temperature of the water.

Why? It takes more heat energy to change the tem-

perature of the water. Thus, the water heats more slowly than the soil does. The difference in the time it takes for land and water to change temperature affects the movement of air above them. During the day, the land heats more quickly than the ocean. Warmer air above the land rises, and cooler air above the water rushes in to take the place of the rising warm air. This air movement is called a **sea breeze**.

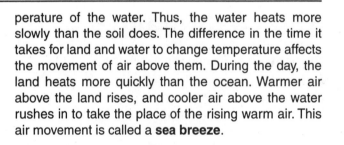

153. Block Out

Purpose To determine how volcanic clouds can lower atmospheric temperature.

Materials white poster board
ruler
clear plastic report cover
8 paper cups
cardboard, the size of the report cover
2 thermometers
timer

Procedure

1. At midday on a sunny day, lay the poster board on a table outdoors or on the ground.
2. Set the paper cups, upside down, on the poster board. Space them so that one cup sits under each corner of the plastic sheet and cardboard, as shown.
3. Read and record the temperature on both thermometers. Then place one thermometer under each cover.
4. After 15 minutes, read the thermometer again.

Results The thermometer under the clear plastic sheet has the higher temperature.

Why? The clear plastic sheet is **transparent**, which means it allows light to pass through. The cardboard does not allow light to pass through, making it an **opaque** object. Normally, the **atmosphere** of the earth is relatively transparent. The clouds formed by some volcanic eruptions contain **opaque** ash particles that block out some of the sun's solar rays. This results in a lowering of atmospheric temperature, just as the opaque cardboard blocking the sun's rays resulted in a lower temperature on the thermometer underneath it.

154. Rain Gauge

Purpose To make and use a rain gauge.

Materials scissors
ruler
2-liter soda bottle
transparent tape
1 cup (250 ml) aquarium gravel or small rocks
tap water
adult helper

Procedure

1. Ask an adult to cut the top off the bottle so that 8 inches (20 cm) remain. Discard the top.
2. Tape the ruler vertically to the side of the bottle with the zero end of the ruler at the bottom, just above the bottle's plastic base, as shown in the diagram.
3. Pour the gravel into the bottle. Then, pour water into the bottle until it reaches the zero end of the ruler.
4. Set the bottle in the corner of your shower stall or bathtub before you take a shower, or outside.
5. After you finish your shower or the rain has stopped, see how high the water is in the bottle.

Results The height of the water depends on the amount of shower water or rain that fell.

Why? The bottle with the ruler attached is a rain gauge. A **rain gauge** is an instrument that can be used to collect falling water. It measures the depth of water that would cover the ground or surface if none of the water drained away or evaporated. The gravel in the bottle weighs down the bottle so that it won't fall over. The water is added so that the water line begins at the zero end on the ruler.

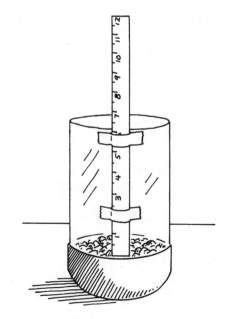

155. Under Cover

Purpose To determine the effect of overhead covering on dew formation.

Materials umbrella
2 sheets of black construction paper
timer

Procedure

NOTE: Perform this experiment on several calm, clear nights during different seasons.

1. Just before sunset, open the umbrella and place it on the ground, as shown in the diagram.
2. Lay one sheet of paper under the umbrella and lay the other sheet of paper on the ground with no overhead covering.
3. After sunset, check the papers every 30 minutes for 2 hours.

Results Water collects on the paper with no overhead covering, but not on the protected paper.

Why? Dew point is the temperature at which dew forms. **Dew** is the water droplets that form when moisture in the air **condenses** (changes to liquid). The black paper cools by losing heat energy. The heat **radiates** (moves away) from the sheets of paper. The uncovered sheet loses enough energy to cool to dew point, so water condenses on its surface. Some of the heat from the covered paper is absorbed by the umbrella and is radiated back to the paper, keeping the paper from cooling to dew point. Clouds, tree branches, and other overhead coverings, like the umbrella, can prevent dew from forming on objects beneath them.

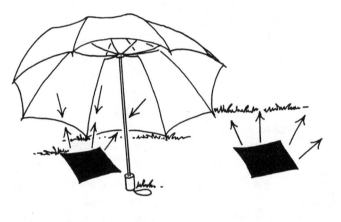

156. Twister

Purpose To demonstrate the shape of a tornado.

Materials two 2-liter soda bottles
tap water
paper towel
flat metal washer with the same circumference as the mouth of the bottles
duct tape
adult helper

Procedure
1. Ask an adult to remove the plastic rings left on the necks of the bottles when the caps are removed.
2. Fill one bottle half full with water.
3. Dry the mouth of the bottle with the paper towel and place the washer over the mouth of the bottle.
4. Place the second bottle upside down on top of the washer.
5. Secure the bottles together with tape.
6. Turn the bottles upside down so that the bottle with the water is on top. Stand the bottles on a table.
7. Place one hand around the lower bottle and the other hand on top of the upper bottle.
8. Support the lower bottle while quickly moving the top of the upper bottle in a small counterclockwise circle.

9. Stand the bottles upright, with the empty bottle remaining on the bottom.

Results The water inside the upper bottle swirls in a counterclockwise direction, forming a funnel shape as it pours into the lower bottle.

Why? The funnel formed by the swirling water is called a **vortex** (a whirling mass of air or water). The vortex formed in the water is the same shape as the vortex formed by a **tornado** (a violently **rotating** funnel cloud that touches the ground). A tornado looks like a swirling funnel hanging down from a dark thundercloud.

157. Boom!

Purpose To determine what causes thunder.

Materials 9-inch (23-cm) round balloon
glove
straight pin

Procedure
1. Inflate the balloon and make a knot.
2. Lay the inflated balloon on a table.
3. Place the glove on one hand.
4. Hold the pin with the gloved hand.
5. Stand at arm's length from the balloon.
6. Stick the pin into the balloon.

Results When the pin is inserted into the balloon, the balloon rips. At the same time a loud popping noise is heard.

Why? When your lungs force air inside the balloon, the rubber stretches and the balloon inflates. The air inside the balloon pushes outward. The stretched rubber pushes the air inside the balloon.

Sticking the pin into the balloon makes a tiny tear. The stretched rubber immediately starts to pull at the tear. At the same time, the **compressed** air rushes out and pushes on the tear. The balloon breaks apart.

As the compressed air rushes through the tear, it expands (moves apart). This quick expansion of air pushes outward against the air surrounding the balloon. This creates sound waves that reach your ears as a popping sound. Thunder is produced in a similar way. As lightning strikes, it gives off energy that heats the air through which it passes. This heated air quickly expands, then cools and contracts. The fast expansion and contraction of air around lightning causes air molecules to move back and forth, which in turn produces sound waves that you hear as **thunder**.

158. Waves

Purpose To demonstrate the motion of water waves.

Materials Slinky
helper

Procedure
1. Lay the Slinky on the floor.
2. Stretch the Slinky between you and your helper.
3. Gently move one end of the Slinky back and forth several times.
4. Change the speed of your back-and-forth movement by increasing and decreasing the distance the Slinky is moved.

Results Waves of motion move from one end of the Slinky to the other. The wave size increases with an increase in the distance that the end is moved.

Why? Waves that move up and down are called **transverse waves**. The highest part of each wave is called the **crest**, and the lowest part is called the **trough**. The movement of the Slinky is a flat version of how water waves look and move from one point to another. Waves move from one end of the Slinky to the other, but the material in the Slinky stays in relatively the same place. Water **molecules**, like the rings in the Slinky, move up and down, but they do not move forward. Only the energy of each wave moves forward.

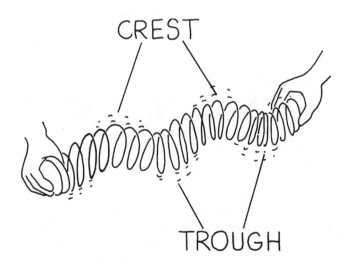

159. Sinker

Purpose To determine how density affects water movement.

Materials 1-cup (250-ml) measuring cup
tap water
⅓ cup table salt
spoon
blue food coloring
2-quart (2-liter) glass container
helper

Procedure
1. Fill the measuring cup with about ¾ cup (200 ml) of water. Add the salt to the water and stir.
2. Add enough food coloring to make the water a very deep blue color.
3. Fill the container half full with water.
4. Observe the container from the side as your helper slowly pours the blue salty water down the side of the container.

Results The colored water sinks to the bottom of the container, forming waves under the clear water above it.

Why? A **density current** is the movement of water due to the difference in the **density** of water. All sea water contains salt, but when two bodies of water mix, denser water (the water with the most salt) will move under the less dense water (the water with less salt).

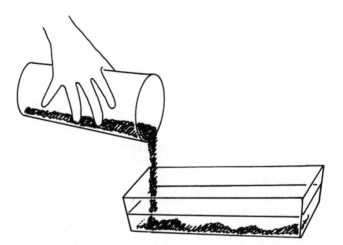

160. Weight Loss

Purpose To demonstrate how density affects the ability to float.

Materials 2-liter soda bottle with cap
tap water
glass eyedropper

Procedure
1. Over a sink, fill the bottle with water to overflowing.
2. Partially fill the eyedropper with water.
3. Drop the eyedropper into the bottle of water. If the eyedropper sinks, remove it, squeeze some of the water out, and drop it back in.
4. Be sure the bottle is full of water, then secure the cap on the bottle.
5. Squeeze the sides of the bottle with your hands.
6. Observe the eyedropper and the water level inside.
7. Release the bottle and observe the movement of the eyedropper and the water level inside.

Results Squeezing causes the water to rise inside the eyedropper, and it sinks. When the bottle is released, the water level lowers inside the eyedropper, and the eyedropper moves upward.

Why? Squeezing the bottle increases the pressure inside, causing water to move into the open eyedropper.

The extra water increases the **density** of the eyedropper. It sinks because the upward push of the water is not great enough to hold up the now-heavier eyedropper. The dropper rises when its density is lessened by the loss of water. Submarines, like the dropper, move up and down in the water due to changes in density. The submarine sinks by taking water into side tanks and rises by blowing that water out.

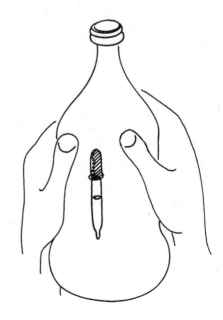

161. What's Up

Purpose   To determine if water pressure is affected by volume.

Materials   2 sheets of newspaper
marking pen
ruler
paper cup, at least 4 inches (9 cm) tall
1-gallon (4-liter) plastic jug
large nail
masking tape
tap water
adult helper

Procedure

1. Place both sheets of newspaper on the edge of a table outside.
2. Make one mark in the center of each sheet of paper.
3. Measure and mark heights of 1 inch (2 cm) and 3 inches (7.5 cm) on the cup and plastic jug.
4. Ask an adult to use the nail to punch a hole in the cup and the jug on the 1-inch (2.5-cm) mark.
5. Cover each hole with tape.
6. Fill each container with water to the 3-inch (7.5-cm) mark.
7. Place the papers side by side and set the edge of each container on the marks in the center of each sheet, with their holes facing in the same direction.
8. Remove the tape from each container.

Results   Water sprays out the same distance from each container.

Why?   The pressure of the water is due to its depth and not to the total volume of the water. Water pressure at a depth of 2 yards (2 m) is the same in a swimming pool as it would be in the ocean. The pressure of the water is due to the amount of water pushing down. Water pressure increases with depth, due to more water pushing down from above.

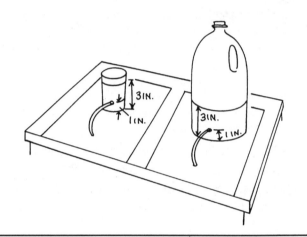

162. Tasty

Purpose   To determine the taste of ocean water.

Materials   2 9-ounce (180-ml) cups
tap water
¼ teaspoon (0.63 ml) table salt
spoon
marking pen

NOTE: Never taste anything in a laboratory setting unless you are sure that it does not contain chemicals or materials.

Procedure

1. Fill each cup half full with water.
2. Add the salt to one of the cups of water and stir.
3. Label the cup containing the salt S.
4. Taste the water in each cup.

Results   The cup marked S tastes salty.

Why?   Ocean water, like the water in cup S, tastes salty because of the salt dissolved in it. A mixture of ¼ teaspoon (0.63 ml) of table salt in 90 ml of water contains about the same amount of salt as ocean water does. Sodium chloride is the chemical name for table salt, which is the most abundant salt in seawater.

163. Salty Water

Purpose To determine how the ocean gets its salt.

Materials pencil
2 paper cups
coffee filter
1 tablespoon (15 ml) soil
1 tablespoon (15 ml) table salt
spoon
sheet of black construction paper
plate
modeling clay
tap water

Procedure
1. Use the pencil to punch 6 holes in the bottom of one of the paper cups.
2. Place the coffee filter inside the cup.
3. In the other cup, mix the soil and the salt together.
4. Pour the soil-salt mixture into the cup with the coffee filter.
5. Place the paper on the plate.
6. Use the clay to make short legs to support the cup above the paper.
7. Add spoonfuls of water until water starts to drain out of the cup.
8. Allow the water to drain. Then let the paper dry.

Results White crystals of salt form on the paper.

Why? As the water flows through the soil, the salt dissolves in it and collects on the black paper. As the water **evaporates** from the paper, the dry salt is left behind. In nature, rainwater dissolves salt from the soil. If this water finds its way to rivers that flow into the ocean, the salt is added to the ocean water.

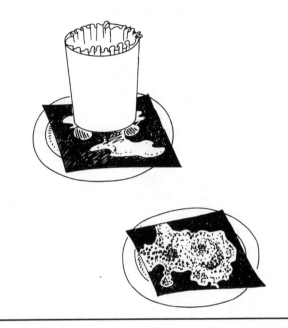

164. Tides

Purpose To determine the effect of centrifugal force on tides.

Materials pencil
7-ounce (210-ml) paper cup
24-inch (60-cm) piece of string
tap water

Procedure
1. Use the pencil to punch 2 holes across from each other beneath the top rim of the paper cup.
2. Tie the ends of the string through each hole in the cup.
3. Fill the cup one-fourth full with water.
4. Take the cup outside.
5. Hold the string and swing the cup around in a horizontal circle above your head several times.

Results The cup turns sideways, but the water stays inside the spinning cup.

Why? The **gravitational** pull of the moon causes the ocean water to bulge on the side of the earth facing the moon. There is another bulge of water on the side of the earth opposite the moon. This second bulge results partly from the **rotation** of the earth. Spinning produces a **centrifugal force** that causes the turning object to tend to fly away from the center around which it turns.

The water in the cup moves outward because of centrifugal force, but the paper cup prevents it from flying away. The **revolution** of the earth around the sun produces a centrifugal force. The earth's rotation about its own axis contributes to this force. The result of this spinning, as well as of the position of the moon and sun, is a bulging of the ocean waters on the earth, called **high tides**. The bulging water is prevented from spinning out into space by the earth's gravitational force.

165. Clean Up

Purpose To demonstrate a way to clean up an oil slick.

Materials clear drinking glass
tap water
6 to 8 washers
empty prescription medicine container,
    large enough for the washers to fit in
24-inch (60-cm) pieces of string
¼ cup (63 ml) cooking oil
small bowl

Procedure

1. Fill the glass three-fourths full with water.
2. Place 2 or 3 washers in the container and tie the ends of the strings around the top of the container. Tie the other ends of the strings together to form a loop.
3. Place the container in the glass of water and support it upright by holding the loop.
4. Continue to add washers until the top of the container is just below the surface of the water. Remove the container and pour out any water, but keep the washers inside.
5. Pour the oil into the glass, then slowly lower the weighted container into the glass.

6. With the loop, support the container so that its top is just below the surface of the oil.
7. When the container fills, raise it, pour its liquid contents into the bowl, and observe the liquid.
8. Continue to fill the container until all the oil is removed from the glass.

Results The first few collections are pure oil, then a mixture of oil and water is collected.

Why? Oil is a very visible **pollutant** (something that makes a substance dirty or impure) of the oceans. Because it floats and does not mix with seawater, it can be retrieved more easily than other pollutants. One method of retrieval is very similar to this method. An oil drum is weighted so that its top is just beneath the surface. The floating oil flows into the drum and is then pumped out.

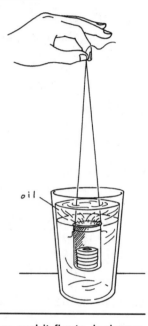

166. Floater

Purpose To demonstrate the position of an iceberg in water.

Materials 3-ounce (90-ml) paper cup
tap water
large-mouthed quart (liter) jar

Procedure

1. Fill the cup with water.
2. Place the cup in the freezer for 2 hours or until the water in the cup is completely frozen.
3. Fill the jar three-fourths full with water.
4. Remove the ice from the cup. To do this, wrap your hands around the cup for 5 to 6 seconds. The warmth from your hands will melt some of the ice, making it easy to remove from the cup.
5. Tilt the jar and slowly slide the ice into the jar.
6. Observe the amount of ice above and below the surface of the water.

Results More ice is below the water's surface than above it.

Why? When water freezes, it expands. Thus the **density** of ice is slightly less than the density of water. As a

result, ice is lighter than water and it floats. Icebergs, like the cup of ice, also float in water. Like all floating ice, most of the iceberg is below the water's surface.

V
Physics

167. Flashlight

Purpose   To determine how a flashlight works.

Materials   flashlight that holds 2 size D batteries
16-inch (40-cm) aluminum foil strip
duct tape
2 size D batteries

Procedure

1. Unscrew the top section (which holds the bulb) from the flashlight.
2. Wrap one end of the foil strip around the base of the bulb holder.
3. Tape the two batteries together with the positive terminal of one touching the negative terminal of the other.
4. Stand the flat, negative terminal of the battery column on the free end of the foil strip.
5. Press the metal tip at the bottom of the flashlight bulb against the positive terminal of the battery, as shown in the diagram.

Results   The light glows.

Why?   The bulb glows when an **electric current** (flow of electric charges) flows through the circuit, which includes the battery, foil strip, and fine wire filament in-

side the flashlight bulb. The movement of the current through the wire filament causes the wire to get hot enough to give off light.

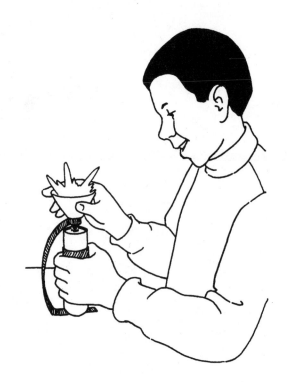

168. Attracters

Purpose   To demonstrate the attraction between unlike charges.

Materials   two 9-inch (23-cm) round balloons
marking pen
two 1-yard (1-m) pieces of thread
masking tape
clean, dry, oil-free hair

Procedure

NOTE: This experiment works best on a cool, dry day.

1. Inflate both balloons and tie their ends. Use the marking pen to label one balloon A and the other balloon B.
2. Tie one thread to the end of each balloon.
3. Tape the free ends of the threads to the top of a door frame so that the balloons hang about 8 inches (20 cm) apart.
4. Stroke balloon A on your hair about 10 times, then gently release it.

NOTE: Leave the balloons hanging for Experiment 169.

Results   The two balloons move toward each other and stick together.

Why?   All **matter** is made up of **atoms**, which have negatively charged **electrons** spinning around a positive **nucleus**. Electrons are rubbed off the hair and collect on balloon A; thus, the balloon becomes negatively charged. Since like charges **repel** (push away) each other, these negative charges on balloon A repel the electrons of balloon B, causing B's surface to be more positively charged. The balloons now have opposite charges, so they are attracted to each other.

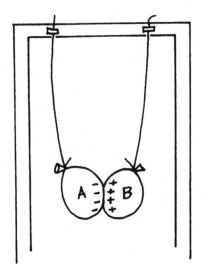

169. Repellers

Purpose To demonstrate the repulsion between like charges.

Materials hanging balloons from Experiment 168
clean, dry, oil-free hair
helper

Procedure

NOTE: This experiment works best on a cool, dry day.

1. Stroke balloon A on your hair 10 times.
2. Hold your balloon as your helper rubs balloon B on your hair 10 times.
3. Gently release the balloons.

Results The balloons move away from each other.

Why? Rubbing both balloons on your hair results in a buildup of negatively charged **electrons** on their surfaces. The balloons move away from each other because they have the same charge and like charges **repel**.

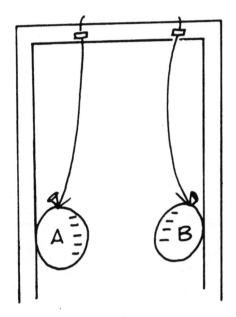

170. Sticky?

Purpose To demonstrate the effect of static electricity.

Materials transparent tape

Procedure
1. Press two pieces of tape onto a table, leaving a small piece hanging over the edge.
2. Hold the ends of the tape and quickly pull both pieces up off the table.
3. Bring the two pieces near each other, but not touching.

Results The pieces of tape move away from each other.

Why? When there is a buildup of **static charges** (stationary electrical charges) in one place, the object is said to have **static electricity**. Pulling the tape pieces from the table causes them to pick up negatively charged **electrons** from the atoms in the table. Both pieces of tape are negatively charged. Materials with like charges **repel** each other.

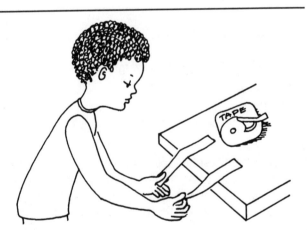

171. Line Up

Purpose To demonstrate how electricity and magnetism are related.

Materials long iron nail
piece of cardboard, 6 inches (15 cm) square
1 yard (1 m) 18-gauge insulated wire
roll of masking tape
6-volt battery
iron filings (purchase at a teacher-supply store)
adult helper

Procedure
1. Ask an adult to use the nail to punch a hole through the center of the cardboard.
2. Wrap the wire tightly around the nail, leaving about 6 inches (15 cm) of free wire on each end.
3. Ask your helper to strip the insulation off both ends of the wire and to insert the wire-wrapped nail through the hole in the cardboard.
4. Make the cardboard sit flat by placing it on the roll of tape. Then attach one end of the wire to either battery terminal.
5. Sprinkle a thin layer of iron filings on the cardboard around the coiled wire.

6. Attach the free wire to the open battery terminal.
7. Observe the pattern made by the iron filings.

CAUTION: The nail and wires will get hot if left connected to the battery. Be sure to interrupt the circuit by disconnecting one wire from one pole.

Results The iron filings form a starburst pattern around the coil of wire.

Why? There is a **magnetic field** around all wires carrying an **electric current**. The iron filings are pulled toward the magnetized nail and form a starburst pattern around the coil of wire.

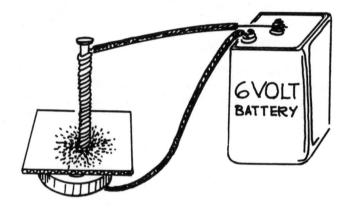

172. Eraser

Purpose To observe how magnets affect recording tapes.

Materials blank cassette tape   strong magnet
cassette recorder   pencil

Procedure
1. Place the cassette tape in the recorder.
2. Record your voice on the cassette tape. (Don't try this experiment with a tape you want to keep.)
3. Rewind the tape in the recorder and listen to your voice.
4. Remove the cassette from the recorder.
5. Use the pencil to rewind the cassette while rubbing the magnet against the tape as it appears. Continue until the beginning of the tape is reached.
6. Place the cassette tape back in the recorder and replay it.
7. Observe the sounds produced.

Results Most or all of your voice will be erased.

Why? The cassette tape contains a magnetic strip wound around two spools. Tiny magnetic particles are randomly scattered throughout the tape. The magnetic particles form no particular pattern on a blank tape. Sound waves entering the microphone of the machine are changed into electrical waves. These waves move magnets that are inside the machine, and the movement of the magnets rearranges the magnetic particles on the tape. Certain positions of the magnetic particles produce the sound of your voice. Rubbing the tape with a magnet causes the magnetic material to be pushed and pulled out of place. Rearranging the magnetic particles erases the sound of your voice. Magnetic recording tapes should be kept away from magnets.

173. Stickers

Purpose To discover what materials are attracted to a magnet.

Materials testing materials: aluminum foil, copper wire, glass marble, iron nail, paper, steel BBs, wooden match
bar magnet

Procedure
1. Lay the testing materials on a *wooden* table.
2. Touch the magnet to, and slowly move the magnet away from, each material.
3. Observe and record which materials cling to the magnet.

Results The iron nail and the BBs are the only materials that cling to the magnet.

Why? One end of a magnet called its north pole is attracted to the earth's **magnetic north pole**. The other end of the magnet is attracted to the earth's **magnetic south pole**. All materials have clusters of **atoms** that like a magnet are **dipolar** (have both a north and a south pole). These clusters are called **domains**. In magnetic materials, many of the domains line up with their north poles pointing in the same direction. The more uniform the arrangement of domains, the stronger the magnetic property of the material. **Nonmagnetic** materials have domains that are arranged haphazardly.

174. More Muscle

Purpose To determine what part of a magnet has the strongest attracting ability.

Materials scissors
ruler
string
bar magnet
masking tape
box of about 100 small paper clips
large bowl

Procedure
1. Cut two 3-foot (1-m) pieces of string.
2. Tie one end of each string to each end of the magnet.
3. Tape the free ends of the strings to the top of a door frame.
4. Adjust the length of the strings so that the magnet hangs in a level position and is at a height that is easy for you to reach.
5. Spread the paper clips in the bottom of the bowl.
6. Raise the bowl so that the magnet touches the paper clips.
7. Slowly lower the bowl.
8. Observe where the clips cling to the magnet.

Results Most of the clinging paper clips are near the ends of the magnet.

Why? All magnets are surrounded by an area called a **magnetic field**. This area is made of invisible lines of force coming out of the north pole of the magnet, around each side, and into the south pole of the magnet. The magnetic force lines are closest together at the poles, which gives the poles the strongest magnetic attraction.

175. Straight Through

Purpose To determine if magnetic forces act through paper.

Materials sheet of typing paper
bar magnet
thumbtack

Procedure

1. Lay the sheet of paper on a *wooden* table.
2. Place the magnet so that its north pole is under the edge of the paper.
3. Position the thumbtack on top of the paper where the paper covers the end of the magnet.
4. Hold the uncovered end of the magnet with your hand and move the magnet from side to side under the paper.

Results The paper is not attracted to the magnet, but the thumbtack is. Moving the magnet caused the thumbtack to move.

Why? Around every magnet is an invisible **magnetic field**. Some materials, such as paper, do not stop or disrupt the pattern of the force field. Materials that allow lines of magnetic force to pass through without any disruptions in the magnetic field are said to be **nonpermeable**. Nonpermeable materials are not attracted to a magnet. The lines of magnetic force pass through the paper with no change in their direction; thus, the paper is nonpermeable and **nonmagnetic**.

176. Floating Boat

Purpose To determine how a heavy ship floats.

Materials scissors
ruler
aluminum foil
20 paper clips
small bucket
tap water

Procedure

1. Cut two 12-inch (30-cm) squares from the aluminum foil.
2. Wrap one of the metal squares around 10 paper clips and squeeze the foil into a tight ball.
3. Fold the four edges of the second aluminum square up to make a small boat.
4. Place 10 paper clips in the boat.
5. Fill the bucket with water.
6. Set the boat on the water's surface in the bucket.
7. Place the metal ball on the water's surface.

Results The boat floats and the ball sinks.

Why? The ball and boat both have the same weight, but the ball takes up a smaller space than does the boat. The amount of water pushed aside by an object equals the force of water pushing upward on the object. The larger boat pushes more water out of its way than does the ball and thus there is enough upward force to cause it to float. Ships are very heavy, but they are large, which increases their **buoyancy**.

177. Bubbler

Purpose To determine what happens to air bubbles in water.

Materials 1-gallon (4-liter) large-mouthed jar
tap water
flexible drinking straw
small balloon

Procedure
1. Fill the jar with water.
2. Place one end of the straw in the water at the bottom of the jar.
3. Inflate the balloon and twist the neck to prevent the air from escaping.
4. Slip the mouth of the balloon over the end of the straw. Hold securely with your fingers.
5. Untwist the balloon and allow the air to escape slowly through the straw.
6. Watch the end of the straw in the water and notice the movement of the air as it exits the tube.

Results Bubbles are formed at the end of the straw. The bubbles rise to the top of the water's surface and escape into the air.

Why? The air bubbles push water out of their way as they emerge from the end of the straw. The weight of the water pushed aside equals the amount of upward force on the bubbles. This force is called **buoyancy**. The air bubbles are so light that they quickly push to the top of the water where they break through the water's surface and mix with the air surrounding the jar.

178. Hanging Bubbles

Purpose To discover how gravity affects the shape of soap bubbles.

Materials small bowl
¼ cup (60 ml) dishwashing liquid
¼ cup (60 ml) water
1 teaspoon (5 ml) sugar
spoon
large empty thread spool

Procedure
1. Place the bowl on a table outdoors. Add the dishwashing liquid, water, and sugar to the bowl.
2. Dip one end of the spool into the mixture.
3. Place your mouth against the dry end of the spool, and gently blow through the hole in the spool.
4. Blow a large bubble, but do not allow it to break free from the spool. Then, place your finger over the hole you blew through to prevent the air from leaking out of the soap bubble, as shown.
5. Study the bubble's shape.

Results A bubble that is slightly pointed on the bottom hangs from the spool. Tiny, threadlike streams of liquid quickly swirl down the sides of the bubble and collect at the bottom, where they form drops and fall.

Why? The **molecules** of dishwashing liquid and water link together to form a thin layer of **elastic** liquid that stretches to surround the air blown into it. **Gravity** pulls the **spherical** bubble downward, forming a slight point at the bottom. The molecules that make up the thin film of the bubble are also pulled downward, causing the bubble's skin to continue to become thinner at the top until it finally breaks.

179. Antigravity?

Purpose To demonstrate overcoming the forces of gravity.

Materials modeling clay
baby food jar
tap water
red or blue food coloring
spoon
drinking straw

Procedure

1. Press a marble-sized piece of clay against the in-side of the bottom of the jar.
2. Fill the jar one-half full with water.
3. Add 3 or 4 drops of food coloring to the water and stir.
4. Slowly lower the straw into the colored water.
5. Push the bottom end of the straw into the clay. The straw can now stand in a vertical position.
6. Quickly turn the jar upside down over a sink.
7. Turn the jar right side up and set it on a table.
8. Observe the contents of the straw.

Results Colored water remains in the straw. The height of the water in the straw is the same as that of the water before it was poured out.

Why? Water **molecules** are attracted to each other. At the surface of the water, the molecules tug on each other so much that a skinlike surface is produced. The air in the straw pushes up on the water when the jar is inverted and water molecules are pulling from side to side. These forces are greater than the downward force of **gravity**; thus, the water remains in the straw.

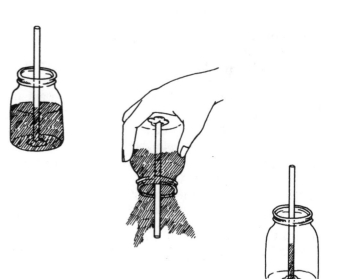

180. Up and Over

Purpose To determine what a siphon is and how gravity affects it.

Materials 2 drinking glasses
tap water
flexible drinking straw

Procedure

1. Fill one glass with water.
2. Bend the straw and place the short end in the glass of water.
3. Suck on the free end of the straw with your mouth until water comes out.
4. Quickly put the end of the straw into the empty glass.

Results The water flows in a steady stream up the straw then down from the higher glass to the lower glass.

Why? A **siphon** allows liquids to flow uphill. It is a device that lifts a liquid up and over the edge of one container and into another container at a lower level. To start the siphoning process, the tube must be filled with water. One way to do this is by sucking the air out of the tube. Air pressure is the result of **gravity** pulling gas **molecules** in the air downward. In the open glass, the air pressure outside the straw pushing down on the surface of the water is great enough to force the liquid up as high as the bend in the straw. Gravity then pulls the water down and out of the straw. Every drop of water that flows out of the straw leaves an empty space inside the straw. Water from the glass is pushed into the straw to fill this space. As long as the upper end of the straw remains below the surface of the water, a steady stream of liquid flows out of the lower end of the straw.

181. Toys and Gravity

Purpose To determine how gravity affects playing paddleball.

Materials paddleball toy

Procedure
1. Hold the paddle in one hand and the ball in the other hand.
2. Pull the ball straight out horizontally from the paddle as far as your outstretched arms or the elastic will allow.
3. Release the ball.
4. Observe the path of the returning ball.
5. Again, pull the ball straight out from the paddle as far as your outstretched arms or the elastic will allow. Raise the ball about 1 foot (30 cm) from its horizontal position.
6. Release the ball and observe its path.
7. Continue to change the position of the ball until its returning path directs it to the center of the paddle.

Results The returning ball often misses the paddle when it is stretched straight out from the paddle. Holding the ball at a height higher than the top of the paddle results in the ball striking the center of the paddle.

Why? The string pulls the ball toward the paddle, but **gravity** pulls the ball straight down. These two forces cause the ball to continue to fall and at the same time move toward the paddle. The result is that the ball moves in a curved path that arches downward. When pulled straight out, the ball's curved path brings it lower than the paddle's handle. The raised ball still moves in a curved path that arches downward, but the new path ends in the center of the paddle.

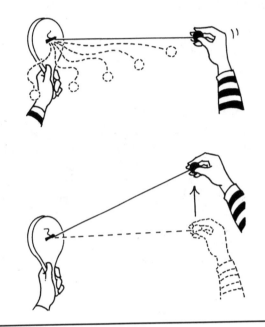

182. Faster

Purpose To demonstrate that heavier things fall faster than lighter things.

Materials paper
book larger than the paper

Procedure
1. Hold the paper in one hand and the book in the other, keeping both waist-high.
2. Drop the book and the paper at the same time.
3. Observe the paper and book as they fall and strike the floor.

Results The book hits the floor before the paper does.

Why? Gravity causes the speed of falling objects to increase at a rate of 32 feet per second (9.8 m per sec) for every second of falling time. All things would fall at this rate, regardless of their **weight**, in a **vacuum**. But air **molecules** in the earth's **atmosphere** push against falling objects and slow their falling rate. Heavier objects, such as the book, push through the air with more force than do lightweight objects, such as the paper. Thus, heavier objects fall through air faster than do lightweight objects.

183. Together

Purpose To demonstrate that gravity pulls all things down at the same rate.

Materials paper
book larger than the paper

Procedure
1. Place the paper on top of the book. Do not have any of the paper hanging over the edges of the book.
2. Hold the book waist-high and drop it.
3. Observe the paper and book as they fall and strike the floor.

Results The book and the paper fall together.

Why? Because **gravity** pulls equally on all objects, the lighter paper and the heavier book both fall at the same rate when air resistance is removed. Experiment 182 showed that the lightweight paper was slowed by the air, while the heavy book was hardly slowed at all. In this experiment, however, the air molecules did not press against the paper because it was on top of the book. So the book and the paper fell at the same rate, just as they would if they were dropped in a **vacuum**.

184. Straw Balance

Purpose To determine how the center of gravity affects a balance.

Materials ruler
drinking straw
marking pen
scissors
small index card
straight pin
2 wooden blocks of equal height and not as wide as the length of the straw
adult helper

Procedure
1. Use the ruler to find the center of the straw and mark the spot with the marking pen.
2. Cut a 1-inch (2.5-cm) slit in the same place on each end of the straw, as shown in the diagram.
3. Cut the index card in half lengthwise and insert the card pieces in the slits in the straw.
4. Ask an adult to punch the straight pin through the center of the straw.
5. Position the two wooden blocks on a table and place the ends of the pin on the edges of the blocks.
6. Move the card pieces out and in until you find the positions that make the straw level with the table.

NOTE: Save the straw balance for Experiment 185.

Results Moving the card pieces causes the straw to drop and rise.

Why? The farther a piece of card is moved away from the pin, the more downward the **rotation** of the straw on that side. The straw is balanced when the position of the cards places the **center of gravity** at the place where the pin is inserted.

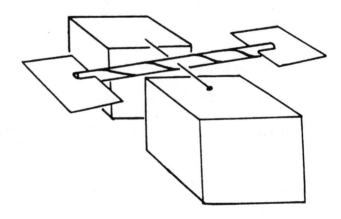

185. Creature Weigh-In

Purpose To compare the weight of a paper creature with that of paper hole-punch circles.

Materials pencil
index card
scissors
straw balance from Experiment 184
paper hole-punch

Procedure

1. Draw your version of a space creature on half of the index card.
2. Cut out the creature and place it on one of the balance's index cards.
3. Punch paper circles from the remaining portion of the index card and continue to place them on the empty card until the straw is level with the table.

Results The end holding the paper creature falls down, but starts to rise as paper circles are added to the opposite card. Too many circles lift the creature above the balancing point.

Why? The downward pull that **gravity** has on an object is called its **weight**. Placing the paper creature on one side of the balance increases the weight on that side. Adding paper circles to the opposite card begins to balance the weight of the creature. When the total weight of the paper circles equals the weight of the paper creature, the balance will be level with the table. The level balance indicates that the pull of gravity is the same on both sides of the balance.

186. Balancing Point

Purpose To locate an object's center of gravity.

Materials scissors
manila folder
paper hole-punch
12-inch (30-cm) piece of string
washer
pushpin
tackboard
ruler
pen

Procedure

1. Cut one side of the manila folder into an irregular shape.
2. Punch five randomly spaced holes in the edge of the paper with the paper hole-punch.
3. Tie one end of the string to the washer and the other end to the pushpin.
4. Stick the pushpin through one of the holes in the paper and into the tackboard.
5. Allow the paper and string to swing freely.
6. Use the ruler and pen to mark a line on the paper next to the string.
7. Move the pushpin to the other holes and mark the position of the hanging string each time. Do this for the remaining four holes.
8. Place the paper on the end of your index finger. Your finger is to be below the point where the lines cross.

Results The paper balances on your finger.

Why? **Center of gravity** is the balancing point of an object. The center of gravity of the paper is the point where the five lines cross. Hold your finger under that point and observe the balance.

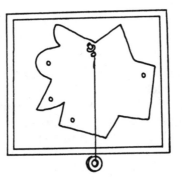

187. Heavy Air

Purpose To demonstrate that air has weight.

Materials modeling clay
pencil
four 12-inch (30-cm) pieces of string
yardstick (meterstick)
three 9-inch (23-cm) balloons (must all be the same size)

Procedure

1. Use the clay to secure the end of the pencil to the edge of a table.
2. Suspend the measuring stick by tying one of the strings to the center of the stick and looping the free ends around the pencil. Adjust the position of the string in order to balance the measuring stick.
3. Use 2 strings to suspend 2 uninflated balloons an equal distance from the center support string. Move the balloons back and forth until the stick and the balloons balance.
4. Inflate a balloon and attach the remaining string. Make a loop with the string ends.
5. Remove one of the uninflated balloons and replace it in exactly the same position with the inflated balloon.

Results The uninflated balloons make the stick balance, but the inflated balloon makes the stick unbalanced.

Why? The stick balances when the downward pull is the same on both sides of the center support string. Replacing the uninflated balloon with an inflated balloon puts extra weight on one side of the stick. The **weight** of the air inside the inflated balloon increases the downward pull on the stick, causing it to move down on that side.

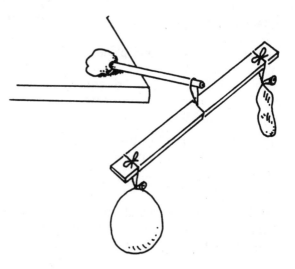

188. Belted

Purpose To make a model of belted wheels.

Materials hammer
large 8-penny nail
2 metal jar lids of equal size
wooden board, 2 by 4 by 12 inches (5 by 10 by 30 cm)
ruler
2 small 6-penny nails
rubber band
marking pen
adult helper

Procedure

1. Ask an adult to use the hammer and nail to make a hole in the center of each lid.
2. Ask your adult helper to attach the lids to the board with the nails, as shown, leaving enough space between the lids and the heads of the nails so that the lids turn easily.
3. Connect the two lids by stretching the rubber band around the outer rims of both lids.
4. Use the marking pen to mark lines on the tops of the lids directly across from each other.
5. Use your hand to turn one lid clockwise so that it makes one complete turn. Observe the marks.

Results Both lids turn clockwise, and the marks return to their original positions at the same time.

Why? The lids and the rubber band act as belted wheels. A belt allows one **rotating** wheel to turn another distant wheel. Wheels connected by a belt rotate in the same direction. Connected wheels of equal **circumference** (the distance around the outside of a circle) turn at the same speed.

189. Flag Raiser

Purpose To determine what a fixed pulley is, and how it makes work easier.

Materials pencil (must be small enough to slide through the hole in the thread spool)
large, empty thread spool
6-foot (2-m) piece of string
blue and red crayons
index card
masking tape
helper

Procedure
1. Place the pencil through the hole in the spool. The spool must turn easily on the pencil.
2. Tie the ends of the string together.
3. Draw and color a flag on the index card.
4. Tape the side with the flag to the string.
5. Place the loop of string over the spool, with the flag hanging at the bottom of the loop.
6. Ask your helper to hold the ends of the pencil, one in each hand at arm's length over his or her head.
7. Pull down on the string opposite the flag.
8. Observe the distance the string is pulled down and the distance and direction the flag moves.

Results The length of string pulled down over the spool equals the distance the flag moves upward.

Why? A **pulley** is a **simple machine** that consists of a wheel, usually grooved, that holds a cord. A **fixed pulley** stays in place; the pulley turns as the cord moves over the wheel, and a load is raised as the cord is pulled. The spool is a fixed pulley that allows you to pull down on the string and raise the flag upward. Placing a fixed pulley at the top of a tall flagpole makes the job of raising a flag easier than if you had to carry the flag up the pole. A fixed pulley makes work easier by changing the direction of the **effort force** (the push or pull needed to move an object).

190. Threads

Purpose To determine how a screw is like an inclined plane.

Materials pencil
ruler
sheet of typing paper
scissors
marking pen
transparent tape

Procedure
1. Draw a right triangle with a base of 4 inches (10 cm) and a height of 6 inches (15 cm) on the paper.
2. Cut out the triangle.
3. Color the diagonal edge of the paper triangle with the marking pen.
4. Tape the triangle to the pencil with the colored edge facing up, as shown in the diagram.
5. Rotate the pencil to wrap the paper tightly around the pencil.
6. Tape the end of the wrapped paper to itself.
7. Count the number of diagonal stripes made by the colored edge of the triangle that is wrapped around the pencil.

Results There are diagonal bands spiraling around the pencil.

Why? A **screw** is an **inclined plane** (a sloping or slanting surface) that is wrapped around a cylinder to form spiraling ridges. Screws look like spiral staircases. A common example of a screw is a wood screw. As this screw **rotates**, it moves into the wood a certain distance. This distance depends on the screw's **pitch** (the distance between the ridges winding around the screw). Each colored band on the paper around the pencil represents a spiral ridge on a screw, which is called a **thread**. Screws with a shorter distance between the threads are easier to turn.

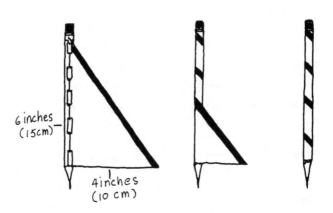

191. Opener

Purpose To determine what a wedge is and how it helps you to do work.

Materials pencil   scissors
                ruler   small book
                thick cardboard

Procedure
1. Draw a right triangle with a base of 4 inches (10 cm) and a height of 2 inches (5 cm) on the cardboard.
2. Cut out the triangle.
3. Place the book on a table.
4. Hold the triangle in your hand, with the 4-inch (10-cm) base against the table and the 2-inch (5-cm) side upright.
5. Support the book so that it does not move forward as you gently push the cardboard triangle under one edge of the book.
6. Observe the direction of motion of both the cardboard triangle and the book.

Results The cardboard triangle moves forward and the book rises upward.

Why? A **wedge** is a **simple machine** shaped like an **inclined plane**. A wedge is actually more like a moving inclined plane. Instead of objects being pushed up its inclined side, the plane moves forward, raising the object. The **effort force** always pushes the wedge forward, and the **load** (the object being moved) moves to the side (perpendicular to the direction of the effort force). The tapered edge of the triangle, like all wedges, enters and makes a path for the larger part of the wedge that follows. Once an opening is made by the point of the wedge, materials are easily pried apart by the gradually widening body of the wedge. It takes less effort to move an object using a wedge than it takes to move it with only your hands.

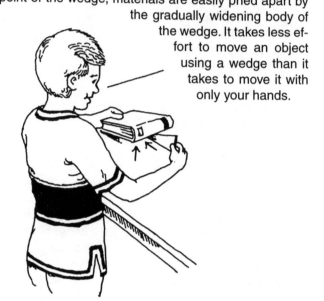

192. Levers

Purpose To demonstrate the effectiveness of a lever.

Materials 4 books
                2 pencils

Procedure
1. Stack the books on a table.
2. Put your little finger under the edge of the bottom book in the stack and try to lift the books.
3. Place one pencil under the edge of the bottom book in the stack.
4. Place the second pencil under the first pencil near the book.
5. Push down on the end of the second pencil with your little finger and try to lift the books.

Results It is very difficult to lift the books with your finger alone, but easy when two pencils are used.

Why? The pencils form a **lever** (a rigid bar that rotates around a fixed point). One of the pencils acts as a **fulcrum** (a point of rotation) for the second pencil. As the distance from where you push down to the fulcrum increases, the easier it is to lift the **load** on the opposite end. Levers are **simple machines** that multiply the force that you apply. This makes moving or lifting large objects easier.

193. Best Spot

Purpose To determine if the position of a lever's fulcrum affects the lever.

Materials ruler
pencil
30 pennies

Procedure

1. Make a lever by laying the 4-inch (10-cm) mark of the ruler across the pencil.
2. Place 10 pennies between the zero end of the ruler and the 1-inch (2.5-cm) mark. This will be called end B.
3. Add and record the number of pennies needed on the opposite end of the ruler end A to lift the 10 pennies.
4. Move the pencil to the 8-inch (20-cm) mark.
5. Add and record the number of pennies needed on end A to lift the 10 pennies.

Results It took many more pennies to lift the 10 pennies when the pencil was at the 8-inch (20-cm) mark.

Why? The ruler and pencil form a **lever**. The pencil acts as the **fulcrum**. In this experiment, the **effort force** was the stack of pennies needed to lift the 10 pennies. The

longer the distance from the point of effort to the fulcrum, the less effort force needed to move the object on the other end.

194. Pumps

Purpose To demonstrate how a wheel can be used as a pump.

Materials drawing compass
ruler
poster board
scissors
round toothpick
eyedropper
tap water
adult helper

Procedure

1. Use the compass to draw a circle with a 4-inch (10-cm) diameter on the poster board.
2. Cut out the circle.
3. Ask an adult to insert about one-third of the toothpick through the center of the circle to form a top.
4. Fill the eyedropper with water.
5. Ask your helper to spin the top.
6. Hold the eyedropper above the top and drop water onto the spinning circle.
7. Observe the movement of the water.

Results The water sprays out in all directions.

Why? The falling water is thrown away from the spinning circle. If you could slow down the motion of the water, you would see that the water leaves the spinning top in a straight line. Spinning materials, if free to move, are thrown off in a straight line. This knowledge was used to

design a **simple machine** to pump water. Water flowing onto a spinning metal disk creates a wheel pump that very effectively pumps water from one spot to another.

195. Inclined

Purpose To determine if an inclined plane makes work easier.

Materials 12-inch (30-cm) piece of string
rubber band
8-ounce (236-ml) glue bottle
2 books
ruler

Procedure

1. Loop the string through the rubber band and attach the string to the top of the glue bottle.
2. Lay the books on a table.
3. Raise the end of one book and rest it on top of the second book.
4. Place the glue bottle on the table near the flat book.
5. Hold the rubber band and lift the bottle of glue straight up and place it on the book.
6. Use the ruler to measure how much the rubber band stretches.
7. Lay the glue bottle at the bottom of the inclined book.
8. Hold the rubber band and pull the bottle until it reaches the height of the flat book.
9. Measure with the ruler how much the rubber band stretches.

Results The rubber band stretches the most when the bottle is lifted straight up.

Why? You lifted the glue bottle to the same height each time, but lifting it straight up took more effort because you were holding the entire **weight** of the bottle. The books form a **simple machine** called an **inclined plane** that helps to support some of the weight of the bottle. You had to pull the bottle up the incline a longer distance to reach the height of the book, but it took much less **effort force**, as shown by the rubber band that stretched less.

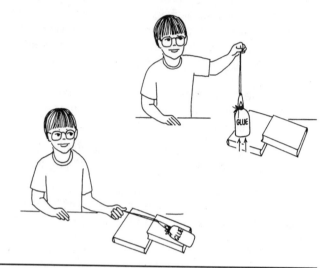

196. Water Prism

Purpose To use water to disperse light into its separate colors.

Materials scissors
heavy paper
ruler
masking tape
clear drinking glass
tap water
chair
sheet of typing paper
flashlight
helper

Procedure

1. Cut a circle from the heavy paper to cover the end of the flashlight.
2. Cut a very thin slit across the circle, stopping about ½ inch (1.25 cm) from each edge.
3. Tape the paper circle to the front of the flashlight.
4. Fill the glass about three-fourths full with water.
5. Place the glass of water on the edge of the chair.
6. Have your helper hold the typing paper near the floor at the edge of the chair.
7. Darken the room and hold the flashlight at an angle to the surface of the water.
8. Change the angle of the flashlight and ask your helper to vary the position of the paper.
9. Look for colors on the paper.

Results A spectrum of colors is seen on the paper.

Why? White light contains all of the **visible spectrum**—red, orange, yellow, green, blue, indigo, and violet. Light can be **dispersed** (separated into the spectrum colors) by passing it through different substances such as water or glass. Dispersion occurs because the different colors of light in white light are **refracted**, or bent, by the substance through which they pass.

197. Starburst

Purpose To demonstrate how a diffracting grating affects light.

Materials lamp
cotton handkerchief

Procedure
1. Remove the shade from the lamp.
2. Stand about 6 feet (2 m) from the glowing bulb.
3. Hold the handkerchief at eye level and stretch it with both hands.
4. Look at the light through the stretched cloth.

Results A starburst of light with dim bands of yellow and orange colors appears around the light.

Why? The cloth acts like a **diffracting grating**, which **disperses** light—separates light into the colors of the **visible spectrum**. Diffracting gratings are made by using a diamond point to cut as many as 12,000 lines per ½ inch (1.25 cm) on a piece of glass or plastic. The spaces between the woven threads in the cloth separate the light, but since the holes in the weave are large, not as many separate colors are seen as one would observe through a diamond-cut grating.

198. Blinker

Purpose To demonstrate the strobe effect of a television picture.

Materials television
pencil

Procedure
1. With the lights on, swing the pencil up and down quickly and observe how it looks.
2. With only the television on, hold the pencil in front of the screen.
3. Quickly swing the pencil up and down 4 to 5 times.

Results In light, the moving pencil produces a continuous blur. In front of the television screen, separate images of the pencil are seen in different places.

Why? Separate images of the pencil are seen in front of the television because the light from the television screen is not constant. Many pictures are flashed on the screen each second. Between the pictures the screen goes black, and the movement of the pencil is not seen. This blinking light gives the illusion that the pencil is moving in slow motion. You do not notice any blinking while watching television because your eyes retain the image of each picture long enough to receive the flashing of the next picture.

199. Sound Blaster

Purpose To demonstrate stereophonic sound.

Materials 36-inch (1-m) piece of string
wire coat hanger
metal spoon
helper

Procedure
1. Wrap the ends of the string around your index fingers.
2. Place your fingers in your ears.
3. Hang the hook of the hanger in the middle.
4. Lean over so that the hanger hangs freely.
5. Ask your helper to use the spoon to tap the hanger several times.

Results A loud chiming sound is heard.

Why? All **sound** is a form of wave motion that is produced when objects **vibrate**. Striking the hanger causes it to vibrate. The vibrations travel through the air and up the string to your ears. This is an example of **stereophonic sound**, which is when different sounds come toward a listener from two different directions. The sounds traveling up the string are slightly different and each sound is directed toward a different ear.

200. Cup Telephone

Purpose To demonstrate how sound travels.

Materials pencil
two 7-ounce (210-ml) paper cups
9-yard (8-m) piece of string
helper

Procedure
1. Use the pencil to make a small hole in the bottom of each cup.
2. Thread the ends of the string through the holes in the cups.
3. Knot each end of the string to keep them from pulling through the holes.
4. Have your helper hold one cup while you hold the other. Hold the cups by placing your thumb and index finger on the rim.
5. Walk away from your helper until the string is stretched tightly between you.
6. Hold the cup to your ear while your helper speaks softly into the other cup.

Results Your helper's words are loud and clear.

Why? **Sound** can travel through solid objects like paper cups and string. Sounds are made by **vibrating** objects. The vibrating vocal cords in your helper's throat cause air **molecules** to vibrate. These vibrating air molecules make the cup vibrate. The vibrating cup makes the string vibrate, and the string passes the vibrations on to your cup. You hear the vibrations as your helper's words.

201. String Music

Purpose To determine how tension in a string affects the sound of stringed instruments.

Materials 6-foot (2-m) piece of strong string
2 buckets with handles (1-quart (1-liter) is large enough)
2 pencils
enough rocks to fill both buckets

Procedure

1. Follow these steps to prepare a model of a stringed instrument:
   ■ Place the string across a table that is about 3 feet (1 m) wide, and tie the ends to the bucket handles so that the buckets hang freely.
   ■ Place the pencils under the string on both edges of the table.
   ■ Fill each bucket half full with rocks.
2. Observe the sound produced as you pluck the center of the string with your fingers.
3. Fill the buckets with the remaining rocks.
4. Again, observe the sound produced as you pluck the center of the string.

NOTE: Keep the model stringed instrument for Experiment 202.

Results Adding more rocks to the bucket produced a higher sound.

Why? Adding **weight** to the buckets increases the tightness or **tension** (condition of being stretched) in the string. As the tension of the string increases, the string **vibrates** faster when plucked, which produces a higher-**pitched** sound.

202. Shorter

Purpose To determine how the length of a string affects the sound of a stringed instrument.

Materials model stringed instrument from Experiment 201
ruler

Procedure

1. The buckets of your stringed instrument should be filled with rocks and the pencils should be near the edge of the table. Pluck the string and make a mental note of the sound heard.
2. Move the pencils about 12 inches (30 cm) apart and pluck the string again. Compare that sound with the sound previously heard.
3. Repeat step 2, moving the pencils about 6 inches (15 cm) apart.

Results The plucked string produces a higher sound when the pencils are closer together.

Why? Moving the pencils closer together has the same effect as shortening the string. The shorter the string, the faster it **vibrates** when plucked, and the higher the **pitch** of the **sound** produced. The same re-

sults occur when a string is shortened on a stringed instrument such as a guitar by holding down a string with one hand while plucking the string with the other.

Glossary

Abrasion: The erosion of a surface by grinding action such as moving sand.

Acid: Substance that turns cabbage indicator red.

Adhesion: The force of attraction between different kinds of molecules.

Altitude: Height.

Anticlines: Folds in rock layers that curve upward.

Aspartame: A sweetener that is about 200 times as sweet as sucrose; trade name of NutraSweet.

Atmosphere: The gases around a planet.

Atoms: The smallest building blocks of matter.

Auxin: A chemical that changes the speed of plant growth.

Barb: The separate stringlike structures of a feather's vane.

Barbules: Growths on each side of a feather's barb.

Barycenter: Center of gravity point between the earth-moon system, which maps out the path of the earth-moon system around the sun.

Base: Substance that turns cabbage indicator blue-to-green.

Body waves: Seismic waves inside the earth.

Bond: (1) The electrical attraction between atoms that connects them. (2) To attach.

Buoyancy: The upward force exerted by a liquid such as water on any object in or on the liquid.

Camouflage: When the color of an organism blends into that of its environment, making the organism difficult to find.

Capillary action: The movement of water or any liquid through a tiny tube.

Casein: Milk protein.

Casts: Waste pellets from earthworms containing undigested soil.

Catalyst: A chemical that changes the rate of a chemical reaction without being changed itself.

Celestial: Of the heavens or sky.

Center of gravity: Point at which an object balances.

Centrifugal force: Outward force exerted by an object moving in a curved path.

Chemoreceptor: A sensory receptor that is stimulated by smell or taste.

Circumference: The distance around the outside of a circle.

Cohesion: The force of attraction between like molecules.

Compress: Push together.

Compression forces: Forces pushing toward each other from opposite directions.

Concave: Crescent-shaped.

Condense: To change from a gas into a liquid.

Conductor: A material that allows electricity, heat, or sound to move through it.

Constellation: A group of stars that, viewed from the earth, form the outline of an object or figure.

Contracts: Gets smaller.

Crater: Bowl-shaped hole.

Crest: Highest part of a wave.

Crust: The outer layer of the earth's surface.

Curd: Solid particles in milk.

Decomposition: The process of breaking down; decay.

Denature: To change something from its natural form.

Density: The scientific way of comparing the "heaviness" of materials.

Density current: Movement of water due to the difference in the density of water.

Dew: Water droplets formed when atmospheric moisture condenses.

Dew point: The temperature at which dew forms.

Diameter: The length of a straight line passing through the center of the circle with both endpoints on the circle.

Diffraction grating: A material that disperses light.

Diffusion: The mixing of molecules because of molecular motion.

Dilate: To get bigger.

Dilute: Thinned out or weakened by adding a solvent.

Dipolar: Having a north and south pole.

Dispersion: The separation of light into its spectrum colors by refraction.

Domain: A cluster of atoms with their north poles pointing in the same direction.

Dormant: Inactive.

Downdrafts: Sinking air.

Earthquake: Shaking of the earth caused by sudden movement of rock beneath the surface.

Eclipse: When one object passes through the shadow of another.

Effort force: The push or pull needed to move an object.

Elastic: Capable of springing back into shape after being stretched or squeezed.

Electric current: Flow of electric charges.

Electron: The negatively charged particle in an atom.

Ellipse: An oval.

Endothermic reactions: A chemical reaction that absorbs energy.

Environment: The natural surroundings of an organism.

Enzyme: Biological catalyst.

Erode: Wear away.

Erosion: The process of being worn away, usually by water or wind.

Escape velocity: The velocity an object must have to escape the earth's gravitational pull.

Evaporation: To change from a liquid to a gas.

Exothermic reaction: A chemical reaction that gives off energy.

Extensor muscle: Muscle that straightens a joint.

Extrusive igneous rock: Igneous rock formed by the solidification of molten rock at or near the earth's surface; also known as extrusive rock.

Eyepiece: The telescopic or microscopic lens closer to your eye.

Fade: To get lighter in color.

Fault: Where the edges of the tectonic plates come together; crack in the lithosphere where surface rocks have slipped up, down, or sideways.

Fixed pulley: A pulley that stays in place.

Flexor muscle: Muscle that bends a joint.

Folds: Bends in rock layers.

Fossils: Traces of the remains of prehistoric animals and plants.

Friction: The resistance to motion between two surfaces that are touching each other.

Fulcrum: The fixed point of rotation on a lever.

Fungi: A group of organisms that lack chlorophyll and must depend on other organisms for food.

Geyser: An inverted funnel-shaped crack in the earth that periodically throws out jets of hot water and steam.

Gravitation: The mutual attraction between objects.

Gravity: Force that pulls toward the center of a celestial body, such as the earth.

Gyroscope: An instrument with a wheel or disk designed to spin around a central axis; used for aiming and steering ships, planes, or spacecraft.

High tides: Point of greatest rise or bulging of the ocean.

Horizon: A line where the sky appears to meet the earth.

Hydraulic mining: Using powerful streams of water to mine metal.

Hydrocarbon: Molecules containing hydrogen and carbon atoms.

Hydrosphere: All of the water on the earth.

Igneous rock: Rock formed from molten rock.

Immiscible liquids: Liquids that are not able to mix together.

Inclined plane: A slanting or sloping surface used to raise an object to a higher level.

Inertia: Resistance to any sudden change in motion or rest.

Insulators: Materials that help prevent temperature changes by slowing the transfer of heat energy.

Iris: The colored muscular circle in the front of the eye.

Joint: Place where bones meet.

Lateral: Sideways.

Lava: Magma that has reached the earth's surface.

Lever: A rigid bar that rotates around a fixed point called a fulcrum; used to lift or move things.

Limestone: A white powder that does not dissolve in water.

Lithosphere: The solid outer part of the earth not including the atmosphere or hydrosphere.

Load: Object being moved.

Lock fault: The point at which two tectonic plates, because of friction, are temporarily locked together.

Luminous: Giving off its own light.

Lunar eclipse: Event that occurs when the moon moves into the earth's shadow.

Magma: Molten rock beneath the surface of the earth.

Magnetic field: Area around a magnet in which the force of the magnet affects the movement of other magnetic objects; made up of invisible lines of magnetic force.

Magnetic north pole: Point on the earth that attracts the north pole of magnets.

Magnetic south pole: Point on the earth that attracts the south pole of magnets.

Matter: Any substance that takes up space and has weight.

Mechanoreceptors: Cells that are stimulated by pressure, touch, or sound.

Meteorite: A stony or metallic object from space that falls through an atmosphere and strikes the surface of a celestial body.

Mirage: Optical illusion due to atmospheric conditions.

Miscible liquids: Liquids that are capable of being mixed.

Molecule: The smallest particle of a substance; made of one or more atoms.

Nadir: Point in the sky below an object on the opposite side of the earth, opposite the object's zenith.

Neutron: The neutral charged particle in an atom.

Nonmagnetic: Materials whose domains are arranged in a haphazard manner and are therefore not attracted to magnets.

Nonpermeable: Materials that allow a magnetic force field to pass through with no disruptions in the magnetic field.

Nucleus: The central part of an atom.

Objective lens: The telescopic or microscopic lens closer to the object being viewed.

Opaque: Does not allow light to pass through.

Orbit: The path of an object around another body; planets moving around the sun.

Ore: Rocks that contain metals that can be mined at a profit.

Osmosis: The movement of water through a semipermeable membrane; movement is toward the side with the least water concentration.

P-waves: Primary earthquake waves. The fastest and most energetic earthquake waves.

Penicillium: A mold from which penicillin, a medicine that kills germs, is made.

Penumbra: The outer, lighter part of a shadow.

Phototropism: Plant growth in response to light.

Physical change: A change that does not produce a new substance.

Pitch: (1) The property of sound that makes it high or low. (2) The distance between the ridges winding around a screw.

Pollutant: Something that makes a substance dirty or impure.

Predator: An animal that lives by killing and eating other animals.

Protein: Large molecules composed of chains of smaller molecules; essential to all living cells for the growth and repair of tissue.

Proton: The positive charge in an atom.

Pulley: A simple machine that consists of a wheel, usually grooved, that holds a cord.

Pupil: The black dotlike opening in the center of the iris that is made larger or smaller by the muscles of the iris.

Radiate: To move away from; movement of heat away from a warm object.

Rain gauge: An instrument that collects rain and measures the depth of rain water that would cover the ground if none drained away or evaporated.

Reflect: Bounce back.

Refract: Bend.

Refracting telescope: A telescope with two lenses, an objective lens and an eyepiece.

Repel: To push away.

Revolve: To move around a central point, as the earth moves around the sun.

Rotate: To spin on one's axis.

S-waves: The slow, secondary earthquake waves.

Saccharin: A sweetener that is about 300 times as sweet as sucrose.

Satellite: A small body moving around a larger body.

Saturated solution: A solution in which no more solute will dissolve.

Scintillation: Twinkling or motion of starlight.

Screw: An inclined plane wrapped around a cylinder to form spiraling ridges.

Sea breeze: Air moving from the sea toward the land.

Seismic waves: Earthquake vibrations.

Semipermeable membrane: A membrane that allows some, but not all, materials to pass through.

Shadow: The dark shape cast upon a surface when something blocks light.

Shaft: The tubelike center of a feather.

Shield volcano: A volcano composed of layers of solidified lava, a wide base, and a large, bowl-shaped opening at the top.

Simple machine: A lever, inclined plane, wheel and axle, screw, wedge, or pulley.

Siphon: A device that lifts a liquid up and over the edge of one container and into another container at a lower level.

Solar eclipse: The event resulting from movement of the earth into the moon's shadow.

Solute: Dissolving material; material that dissolves in a solvent.

Solution: The combination of a solute and solvent.

Solvent: Dissolving medium; the material in which a solute dissolves.

Sound: A form of wave motion produced when objects vibrate.

Space: The partial vacuum separating celestial bodies.

Sphere: Ball shape.

Spinal cord: The large bundle of nerves that runs through the discs of the spine.

Stalactite: A deposit shaped like an icicle, hanging from the roof of a cave.

Stalagmite: A deposit shaped like an upside-down icicle, building up from the floor of a cave.

Static charge: Stationary electrical charges.

Static electricity: A buildup of static charges in one place.

Stereophonic sound: Different sounds coming toward a listener from two different directions.

Sucrose: Table sugar.

Sunspots: Temporary, dark, relatively cool blotches on the sun; magnetic areas on the sun.

Surface tension: The tendency of liquid molecules to cling together at the surface to form a skinlike film across the surface of the liquid.

Suspension: A mixture of two materials: one does not dissolve in the other, but temporarily stays suspended in the liquid until gravity pulls it down.

Synclines: Folds in rock layers that curve downward.

Tectonic plates: Huge, moving pieces of the lithosphere.

Tension: The condition of being stretched.

Thread: The spiral ridge on a screw.

Thunder: Sound waves produced by the fast expansion and contraction of air molecules around lightning.

Tiltmeter: An instrument that measures the tilting of the ground.

Tornado: A violently rotating funnel cloud that touches the ground.

Transparent: Allows light to pass through.

Transverse waves: Waves that move material up and down or side to side as the energy of the wave moves forward.

Trough: Lowest part of a wave.

Tyndall effect: Reflection of light by particles in a suspension.

Umbra: The dark inner part of a shadow.

Updraft: Rising air.

Vacuum: Space with nothing in it.

Vane: The part of a feather excluding the shaft.

Velocity: Speed.

Vibrate: To move quickly back and forth.

Visible spectrum: The colors found in white light: red, orange, yellow, green, blue, indigo, and violet.

Volcanologist: A scientist who studies volcanoes.

Vortex: The funnel shape of a tornado; a whirling mass of air or water.

Weathering: The breaking down of rocks into smaller pieces by natural processes.

Wedge: A machine shaped like an inclined plane that acts like a moving inclined plane.

Weight: The downward pull that gravity has on an object.

Weightlessness: A zero pull of gravity.

Whey: The liquid part of milk.

Xylem: Tiny tubes in the stalk of a plant and leaf stem, which transport water and food to the plant's cells.

Zenith: The point in the sky directly above an object; opposite the object's nadir.

Index